The Bigger Bang
Growth of a Financial Revolution

An outline of the events which unpredictably prepared the way for the so-called 'Big Bang' of October 1986. How something originally conceived as a reform of the London Stock Exchange developed into a programme of radical change affecting all the City's financial institutions — a fundamental revolution which is still in progress.

Also published by Waterlow

How the City of London Works
An Introduction to its Financial Markets
by William M. Clarke

How the City Works Cassette Series
A series of ten audio cassettes on City institutions
edited and introduced by William M. Clarke

The Second Wave
Japan's Global Assault on Financial Services
by Richard W. Wright and Gunter A. Pauli

Services
Driving Force of the European Economy
by Gunter A. Pauli

For further details write to
Waterlow Publishers,
27 Crimscott Street, London SE1 5TS
Tel. 01-232 1000

G. H. Webb, CMG, OBE

Director, Management Development Centre,
City University Business School, London

The Bigger Bang
Growth of a Financial Revolution

WATERLOW PUBLISHERS

First edition 1987

Waterlow Publishers
Oyez House, PO Box 55
27 Crimscott Street
London SE1 5TS
A division of Hollis Professional and Financial Services PLC

ISBN 0 08 033100 9

British Library Cataloguing in Publication Data

Webb, G.H.
The bigger bang: growth of a financial revolution.
1. Stock Exchange (*London*)
I. Title
332.64'24212 HG4577

Printed in Great Britain by
Dramrite Printers Ltd, Southwark, London SE1

Table of Contents

Preface and Acknowledgements

My present close interest in City affairs dates from my appointment to the staff of the City University in October 1985. This was just a year before Big Bang: the fuse had been lit, and the period of waiting was an interesting moment in the long and proud history of the City. My own background was a very different one: thirty-odd years of administrative and political work, much of it abroad, with the Colonial Service and later the Foreign Service. Physically, the distance between Whitehall and the City is a short one, a mile or two: culturally it is much further. For me, the transfer from the one sphere to the other felt at first like a posting to a small but important foreign country, the dynamism of which stemmed from its largely immigrant workforce, particularly that part of it employed in various skilled activities in a unique financial services industry.

On arrival I found a general air of expectation, not unmixed with foreboding. Well informed inhabitants explained readily, but not always articulately and never with enthusiasm, that great changes were impending in their traditional economic structure. The implications were thought to be obscure but serious. It appeared that a revolution, popularly called Big Bang, was due on 27 October 1986. It was being imposed not from below but from above. It was disconcertingly out of keeping with the way the City had normally been run. As to its desirability, opinion varied. Some said it was bound to enhance the City's languishing international competitiveness: others, that it would open the gates to foreign giants who would stride in and eat the natives alive. A few feared that it would have the effect of destroying the valued club-like intimacy and integrity of City professionalism: most admitted that those qualities had already been eroded by increasing cosmopolitanism and the impact of new technology.

It was generally agreed that Big Bang was a logical move in the direction of politically fashionable 'de-regulation': however, cynics suspected that the upshot, paradoxically, would prove to be a burdensome 'self-regulation' through a mass of new rules even then being drafted to meet the doubtfully practicable ideals of 'investor protection': if so, the effect might well be to discourage innovation and even to drive abroad the City's most dynamic markets, in foreign exchange and Eurobonds. All acknowledged that 27 October 1986 would mark the end of a chapter in the history of the Stock Exchange: it was clear to the far-sighted that it must also mark the beginning of a new era for every financial institution in the City. However, on the eventual implications, and even on what would happen on 28 October, those with most experience were commonly the most reluctant to prophesy.

Their reluctance was well founded. Uncertainties about the future were justified, and have been vindicated by events so far. Nor have we yet reached the point when crucial longer-term questions implicit in those uncertainties can be answered. A year after Big Bang, we know vastly more than we knew a year before it, but we are only learning as we go along, and cannot have much assurance of what is round the next corner. This book does not attempt to describe the way ahead – and should not be trusted if it did.

What it does is explain the stages by which we reached the position in which we now find ourselves. We have arrived here as much by chance as by skilful navigation, yet it has not been a process of drift. During several recent years of change, the City's institutions have been gradually but positively prodded into new courses. So many of those prods had been administered before October 1986 that when Big Bang occurred it was almost an anticlimax. Behind the movement to reform were various forces – powerful bodies such as the Bank of England and the Department of Trade and Industry, influential individuals such as Professor Gower, Sir Nicholas Goodison and Sir Kenneth Berrill. However, a master plan was lacking. The leading instigators of change were far from unanimous. That there still remain sharp divisions over principles is demonstrated by the continuation of fierce and impatient argument about the restrictiveness of 'polarisation' for financial advisers, about whether 'PINCs' constitute a 'collective investment scheme' in the eyes of the law, and about many other new concepts. Perhaps most worryingly, there has been no expressed strategy regarding the prudent limits to 'globalisation': the apparent aim has been to internationalise London's financial services industry, but as de-regulation has swept away the barriers between institutions, new and unlooked-for consequences begin to loom, for instance an obvious threat of foreign takeovers at the heart of Britain's core domestic areas such as life assurance companies and clearing banks.

Amid this welter of viewpoints and lack of coherent planning, it was not easy for a newcomer to the City to obtain clear and objective guidance as to what was going on, though I did derive benefit from attending two lectures in 1986 to private audiences. One was by Sir Kenneth Berrill, Chairman of the Securities and Investments Board, the other by Mr E.E. Ray, a member of that Board. Both speakers illuminatingly outlined the progression of events which led to the situation as it then was. Otherwise I did not find many accounts, in the linear and descriptive terms that I needed, which were not either so simplified as to be useless or so technical as to be incomprehensible. I therefore wrote my own account, for non-specialists like myself. It reflects many conversations with City practitioners, and far more press items – from the *Economist*, the *Financial Times* and other serious newspapers – than can possibly be acknowledged; but the shape is wholly of my own making.

The aim is simple: to explain the stages in which the present process of reform fortuitously came about, and briefly to hint where it may be leading us. A shorter narrative could not do justice to the subject, which is complex. Indeed it was tempting to write at greater length, covering trends in the early 1970s such as Competition and Credit Control (CCC), which was a move towards 'de-cartelisation' and arguably a prelude to events that are happening now – and those events too, changeable and half-formed though they are, could justify much fuller explanation than I have attempted. However, precisely because the present position is so fluid, a weightier book than this would be premature: the extraordinary aftermath of Big Bang, the wider upheaval of which the Stock Exchange's reforms were only a part, is still proceeding daily. Even the implementation in full of the Financial Services Act 1986 has had to be deferred well into 1988, and it will be later still before the impact of the new legislation, including its plethora of subordinate rules, can be reliably judged.

Meanwhile, a deliberately limited account may be of use to the general and the professional reader alike, providing a perspective in which the ceaseless flow of new developments can be better assessed. I am grateful to various friends who have kindly read and commented on my text: above all I am grateful to Sir Peter Graham (Chairman of the Standard Chartered Bank, and of the Crown Agents, and also of the Council of the City University's Business School) for encouraging me to write *The Bigger Bang*, and for introducing me to my publishers.

October 1987 *G.H. Webb*

Introduction

We are stuck with the term 'Big Bang', but it is misleading. It suggests a single important event, at one blow changing a prevailing situation into something else. Actually, even for the Stock Exchange, the recent reform of which has helped to trigger the changes elsewhere, the process was by no means as simple as that. As for the City as a whole, the great upheaval it is experiencing, if it can be called a 'Bang' at all, is far bigger, amounting to a legal, structural and economic revolution with far-reaching consequences. It is still rumbling on, and no one can with certainty predict its duration or its outcome.

As soon as the prospect of radical change dawned on the institution most affected, the Stock Exchange, it was inevitable that a nickname would be found for it; by 1984 attention was focussing on a date in late 1986, when most of the new rules for that market were expected to take effect simultaneously. In that limited context, the term 'Big Bang' made a kind of sense: it was incidentally derived from a theory propounded in 1927 by a Belgian astrophysicist, Georges Henri Lemaitre, that our universe had originated in a vast explosion. The expression was probably first applied to impending events in the Stock Exchange in a letter of 1983 from its Chairman to its members, asking if they would prefer their fixed commissions to be reduced progressively or abolished at a stroke. In 1984 it was more publicly used in a speech by the Governor of the Bank of England, and it soon entered common parlance.

It did not follow, of course, that the impending process it described was always understood. Most people outside the City and many within it found the implications of the intended reforms obscure. Still, it was impossible to avoid the feeling that something important was afoot, a feeling sharpened by the realisation that although British manufacturing was in recession, London's financial services industry was booming, and its invisible earnings were a crucial factor in the national economy. In any case, major events in the Square Mile are always headline news; the City's mystique — often distorted one way or another by ignorance, envy or pride — is all too apt to attract notice, the more so given the increasingly wide public interest, in Britain, in share ownership and also in financial institutions generally.

The popular press might therefore have been expected to give the Big Bang substantial and even accurate coverage, but journalists seem to have found the subject too intractable to convey effectively. Admittedly Stock Exchange procedures are in themselves unexciting, and the proposed reforms looked technical and, in their implications, problematical: also a time-scale of two or three years is a long one for sustaining interest. Popular newspaper coverage was therefore quite inadequate, and the question of structural reform was heavily overlaid by more sensational topics, of which the City happened just then to provide an abundance — financial scandals, political controversies, excessive salaries, cynical headhunting and violent takeover battles. Such subjects, natural news material, served to highlight various recent developments such as the scale of remuneration now earned by some dealers and fund managers; but so far from explaining the background to Big Bang, they actually obscured it.

For sophisticated newspaper readers the coverage available was more helpful. In the City, professional people, often with great anxiety, could watch what was happening to their own firm, or could speculate about what might happen. They could also study technical analyses and forecasts, not always objective, of which a great number were published. However, the conclusions of analysts and financial journalists were necessarily tentative and frequently contradictory, which is not surprising given the fluidity of the situation and the wholly new factors in being, such as the unprecedented mobility of money and the immeasurable potential of the latest electronics. Until the morning of 27 October 1986, indeed after that, no one could be sure what the impact of the new procedures on the Stock Exchange would be: even now, a year later, though certain obvious changes have occurred, it is too soon for certainty. As for the wider consequences of the City's financial revolution, of which the Stock Exchange's Big Bang was a key part but only a part, it will be years before a definitive picture emerges.

Meanwhile there is a clear need for an objective account, as free as possible from the technical jargon of economics, accountancy or computer science. It should explain factually how the slow-burning fuse for Big Bang in October 1986 came to be lit, and, more speculatively, some of the immediate implications of the new structures created by the Financial Services Act 1986. This present essay, essentially descriptive rather than analytical, aims to meet that need. It does not aspire to answer longer-term questions; these, though crucial and exciting, are still unanswerable.

Part One: The Scene as It Was

The Uncharacteristic Revolution

Although the reform of the Stock Exchange is only a symptom of the de-regulatory process current throughout the western world, and only a part of the general upheaval in the City of London, the Big Bang of 27 October 1986 deserves study, for three reasons:

(1) it represented a more radical development than any comparable step taken in any other country;

(2) it served as a catalyst for the wider changes now under way in this country;

(3) it was a thoroughly untypical manifestation of the way the City of London had customarily operated.

London, for earlier generations the undisputed centre of world finance and still today a leading market, had been sustained by institutions which had developed gradually, piecemeal over many years, without exposure to any sudden massive structural shock. This was in keeping not only with the traditions of the City itself but with the pragmatic character of the British people, empirical and disinclined to ideology and logic. Since the Big Bang revolution was a bold and drastic step, controversial in conception and designed to be largely fulfilled in a single convulsion, it was in essence distinctly un-British, and certainly uptypical of the City. As such, it occasioned profound misgiving among those most directly affected. The City professionals who operated the old order of things, could see that it was creaking, but were far from agreement as to how it could be overhauled.

During the run-up to October 1986 they were able to judge the sweeping nature of the comprehensive restructuring about to take place: what they doubted was whether those who had taken the first step in 1983 had had any conception of the eventual consequences. It was natural that people standing to lose their livelihood if their firms proved uncompetitive in the new conditions, of if they themselves failed to adapt to the impersonal pressures of computer-driven markets, should incline to cynicism. For many of them it was as if contractors, called in to modernise a famous old building, had determined on structural 'improvements' without recognising that to modify a load-bearing wall or remove the keystone of an arch is to risk collapse.

Nearly twelve relatively trouble-free months after Big Bang, it is well to remember that shortly before it occurred a sense of scepticism was widespread. For instance a poll conducted at the time by a leading firm of chartered accountants suggested that barely 20% of all British and foreign securities firms in the City believed that oversight by the Securities and Investments Board (SIB), a central provision of the Financial Services Bill, would work. Among many anxious questions then being asked, and still relevant, were:

(1) If commissions for stockbroking are reduced, while the number of competitors is increased, now can profits remain adequate?
(2) How can vaunted 'de-regulation', which supposedly provides freer operating conditions, be reconciled with the intrusive new mass of rules to be imposed when the Financial Services Bill becomes law?

To the first question, about profitability, it is still too soon to give an answer: the generally bullish tone of the stock market has effectively disguised the worst-case potential (while by no means assuaging the anxiety of management regarding the dangerous 'inelasticity' of the cost of premises, technology and staff). To the second question, about rules, the answer is merely deferred, well into 1988, owing to prolonged delays in getting the self-regulatory apparatus, provided for by the Act of 1986, into working order. Both these doubts therefore remain real, and with them the fear that eventually only the most heavily capitalised firms — 'deep pockets', many of them foreign — will prosper in the intensely competitive but ponderously bureaucratic conditions that are being created.

On the other hand, historically, root and branch reform, especially when most needed, is seldom a comfortable process.

At least Big Bang was extremely well timed in two important respects:

(1) The Banks had become very ready to participate. In the 1970s they had been engrossed in the business of international lending. However the 'sovereign debt crisis' of 1982 had disenchanted them with this activity, and by the mid-1980s they were attracted by the opportunity to enlarge the securities side of their operations.

(2) There had recently been great advances in the application of computer science. It followed that any financial centre that was motivated to equip itself with the latest systems would find itself, for a time, technically ahead of the world. This has happened to London. A spokesman for Chase Manhattan Securities, a firm with experience both of New York's previous de-regulation and of London's Big Bang, has aptly said that the electronics of 1975 and of 1986 can no more be compared than the weaponry of the first and second World Wars. London has suddenly become the pace-setter.

Whether the planning was shrewdly far-sighted, or the timing was merely fortuitous, the year or two preceding Big Bang acquired a galloping momentum. The stimulus arose not from the sort of artificially-generated reform which can be examined in isolation; rather, the whole process was a symptom of worldwide change. For some fifteen years London institutions and firms had been gradually adapting to the increasing international-mindedness of the investors and traders whom they served, and had dealt more and more across national frontiers. Owing to this widening outlook, and to some extraordinary technological advances which have been both a stimulus and a means to 'globalisation', the Big Bang process, which started with just one technical reform in the Stock Exchange's Rule Book, was destined to be swiftly transformed into a general upheaval.

The Fevered City

Unfortunately, various other upheavals were taking place in the City at the same time: to a small extent these were connected with Big Bang, but for the most part they were not. Yet they combined to distract public attention from the highly important technical actualities of the impending revolution to the sensational but comparatively trivial nature of newsworthy but unrelated events.

The most conspicuous example, of which there seemed to be a sudden surfeit, was take-over bids. The flamboyance of certain oversized figures behind these, the bitter disputes engendered and grossly 'knocking' advertising that ensued, guaranteed wide publicity. The only relevance to the Big Bang was political, through the public projection of a greedy not to say squalid atmosphere, and the related erosion of confidence in business ethics. There is a common tendency in Britain, in marked contrast to the general attitude in the United States, for great wealth to be resented more than admired. In this respect, the recent take-over mania, even when traceable to the ambitions of industrialists rather than to the machinations of their City intermediaries, has done much to provoke a damaging public cynicism, as well as to fuel left wing political antagonism against the standard target of 'the City' — by which is meant the whole pattern of financial institutions largely but not exclusively centred in the historic Square Mile. The radical modernisation of those same financial institutions, however important to the nation, cannot compete for popular attention with the gladiatorial drama of bid and counter-bid. Both are of course eclipsed by any major scandal — whether bankruptcy, fraud or corruption — and it was also the misfortune of the City to throw up several such cases during the present Conservative government's term of office. These cases undoubtedly influenced the government's intention to set up a stringent apparatus of controls under the Financial Services Act 1986 (FSA).

The political vulnerability of the City is a highly important consideration, and can depend as much on image as on fact, given the self-evident divisiveness of a national economy that manifests on the one hand a conspicuously flourishing financial sector with high individual rewards, and on the other a more stagnant industrial base with high unemployment. It is in this context that attention is periodically drawn by politicians, clerics and journalists to 'obscene' salaries gained by young dealers in the City. This is indeed a striking new phenomenon, but it antedates the run-up to Big Bang and was originally due to unrelated factors, notably London's worldwide dominance in the booming Euromarket, the profitability of London-based foreign exchange dealing, the recent concentration of some five hundred foreign banks in the City, and the consequential internationalisation of salary levels in the financial services industry. This has also triggered an upsurge in property values for domestic and office premises alike, in and around London.

It is true that from 1984 the impending Big Bang accentuated these inflationary tendencies, and increased the already urgent demand for staff with premium skills, such as fund managers, market-makers and computer programmers. But the unscrupulous head-hunting that is now prevalent, with its lavish financial inducements, had already been widespread. These manifestations of excess make news and have social and political impact, but are actually less interesting than the causes that underlie them.

In simplified terms these causes have been twofold:

(1) From 1979, when foreign exchange controls were removed, there was a great expansion in the City's flourishing money markets, and it was unconnected with the Stock Exchange.

(2) From 1984, when some of the implications of the impending Big Bang began to be unmistakable, an intense effort was made by some British and overseas banks and securities firms to buy themselves favourable positions from which to exploit the opening up and transformation of the Stock Exchange as soon as this should happen in late 1986.

The second manifestation above, the rush for acquisition, had three main ingredients:

(1) The first was a marked sense of vulnerability (including a readiness to sell out) on the part of firms and individuals that felt unready for radical overhaul, including adaptation to new technology.

(2) The second was a correspondingly strong drive on the part of large expansionist firms, to acquire staff and premises in a hurry, competitively. This in turn created two particular pressures, of a kind with which the City was only just beginning to be familiar:

   (a) Personnel with appropriate skills were procured by offers of very high remuneration — many individuals, and several entire teams, being induced to switch firms in a manner absolutely at variance with traditional City practice, but now defended under colour of 'market forces'.

   (b) Premises had to be found with space for 'Large Open-Area Floors' (LOAFs): it became normal to plan to accommodate a hundred or more dealing staff, with their electronic work units, in a single room. This led some firms to look outside the crowded City itself, for space in the Docklands or in central London. This trend eventually galvanised the City Corporation into making urgent provision for an unprecedented rate of in-filling and new development in the Square Mile.

(3) The third element in the acquisitive rush was a bonus spin-off for members of 'ancillary' professions. Just as the growth of Euromarket dealing with its proliferation of new lending devices had produced a dramatic expansion of City solicitors' firms to handle new loan instrument business, so the Big Bang generated a great deal of new work for chartered accountants. For instance, one major firm in 1986 placed no fewer than sixty consultants on prolonged attachment in a single merchant bank, and forty in another, to correlate and rationalise the computer systems of those firms, without which they would have been unable after 27 October to manage the volume of electronic business. Another highly competitive demand area, of course, was in the marketing of computer equipment and software, since it soon became self-evident

that a major aspect of the financial revolution, and one critical for commercial success or failure, would be the new technology.

In these various ways the tone of the City had by 1986 changed markedly, with symptoms of excitement amounting to hysteria. This overheated atmosphere communicated itself through the media to public attention, and became vaguely associated with an expected event conveniently dubbed 'Big Bang' but in truth very imperfectly understood. Even in the City, where many professionals in financial institutions are surprisingly narrowly focussed on their particular patch, the original chain of causation that lay behind the revolution was commonly overlooked. It had all in fact begun with a narrow, parochial reform of Stock Exchange procedure, a seeming technicality which few would have thought capable of triggering, as it did, the far-reaching changes that ensued.

Part Two: Sudden Change

The First Move

Traditionally, the City of London's financial institutions (not just the Stock Exchange but other trading exchanges, discount houses, insurance companies, banks and merchant banks, etc), though supervised by the Bank of England and other authorities, and subject to the law of the land, were largely self-regulating. Within these institutions, and in their mutual transactions and relationships with member firms, a multiplicity of rules and conventional practices had evolved. The system was conservative, but it worked. To be sure, by the 1970s it was open to the criticism that it depended unduly on informal sanctions and personal relationships reflecting the old 'club' atmosphere of the City, and that it was ill-suited to modern conditions — the infusion of foreign banks, the emergence of short-term money markets, in short the new internationalism and the revolution in communications. With hindsight, it can be seen that the whole apparatus needed shaking up, but this was less clear at the time. Thus when the first preliminary jolt occurred it was not perceived as such.

The great measures of reform that culminated in the Big Bang of October 1986 had their inconspicuous but directly traceable beginnings in 1978 in a complaint about one small part of the City's traditional machinery, namely the 'minimum commissions' charged by brokers on the Stock Exchange. (Incidentally the title 'Stock Exchange' covers not merely the London institution but its affiliates in Birmingham, Bristol, Liverpool, Manchester, Glasgow, Belfast and Dublin.)

It is an illustration of the extent of the change that followed, with the distinction abolished between stockbrokers and stockjobbers (as defined below) and the whole system of fixed commissions swept away, that it is now becoming necessary to explain what 'minimum commissions' meant. They were the fixed rates of commission that stockbrokers charged their clients on all transactions, under Rules dating from 1912. Significantly, fixed commissions on the New York Stock Exchange (NYSE) had been abolished in 1975, in the New York equivalent of Big Bang, 'Mayday'. It now seems obvious that London would be obliged to follow suit, or to lose business to New York, but curiously this was not apparent at the time to a majority of the Council of the Stock Exchange itself; their conservatism made the matter of abolition an issue of hard-fought principle when it should have become no more than a reluctant but logical routine step.

Rates of commission in London varied, of course, according to the scale of transaction. It is a sufficient approximation to say that at the time that minimum commissions came under fire, rates for private clients typically ranged from 1.65%, for deals under £7000, down to 0.55%, for deals between £15,000 and £130,000. For institutional clients the commission was lower, averaging 0.4% on all institutional deals but descending to a bottom rate of 0.3% on deals over £600,000. It needs stressing that the role of the stockbroker, for which he was charging, was not merely to carry out his client's buying and selling instructions and to take responsibility for settlement procedures but to offer 'services', which might include advice on a whole range of investment topics, based on systematic research and analysis.

However, rates in London were undeniably too high. What amounted to a cartel was in operation. This is demonstrated by three indicators. First, after 1975 New York rates had come down to an average of 0.3% on all institutional deals, commonly dropping to 0.15%, which was often in effect eroded further by discounts and services. Second, in competitive manoeuvring in 1986 shortly before Big Bang several institutional brokers in London voluntarily reduced their charges to an average of 0.28% (particularly on a basis known as 'continuation', where major clients are permitted to lump a number of lesser transactions into one). Third, since Big Bang all rates for institutional clients have fallen.

The first move came in 1978 when some institutional investors complained about the unwarrantably high minimum commissions charged by brokers on their transactions. To the question why this complaint had not been raised at any time since 1912, there are various and sufficient answers:

(1) *A matter of muscle.* In the first half of the twentieth century some 75% of deals handled by the Stock Exchange were for private clients. These were dominant, and institutional investors were not.

(2) *A matter of scale.* It followed that institutional investment was the exception rather than the rule, until this began to be changed by social developments after the second World War, with a great rise in the importance of pension funds and benevolent funds. Large scale transactions then began to assume great weight as a percentage of all trading, and it was argued that obvious economies of scale should be reflected in steeper reductions in commission.

(3) *A matter of efficiency.* At the same time, the Stock Exchange's service to institutional investors seemed to be becoming not more but less effective. This was because the much larger 'trades' being made after 1945 involved a larger risk for the stockjobber (in his role as a principal, operating as a wholesaler in a range of stocks, in a 'pitch' on the floor of the Exchange), if he miscalculated market trends. The jobber came to realise that to meet that risk he required a larger capital base, and one way to achieve this capitalisation was by merger. Accordingly the number of jobbing firms on the Exchange contracted between 1945 and 1982 from 100 to 15, which included 10 small ones, and even this contraction was inadequate. The consequence was significant in terms of liquidity. When an intended deal exceeded the capital base of the jobber, he could not take it on: the client's broker had to split the deal and go round the jobbers' pitches. The result was delay and comparative inefficiency.

(4) *A matter of recent precedent.* This has already been mentioned. It was the abolition of minimum commissions in New York that inevitably presaged a parallel step in London.

It followed that the broker's minimum commission, which could be justified in 1912 as the agent's reward, or as a compensation for the prohibition against entering the jobber's field as a 'market-maker' (under the 'single capacity' rule which is more fully discussed later), had begun by the mid-1970s to resemble a restrictive practice. Therefore, when the complaint was made, the Labour government of the day invited the Office of Fair Trading (OFT) under Mr (later Sir) Gordon Borrie, who is still its Director General, to investigate the Stock Exchange's Rule Book. Only recently (in 1976) had the powers of the OFT been extended to include service industries as well as manufacturing industry. An investigation was accordingly initiated. In due course the OFT decided that there were sufficient grounds, in the public interest, to refer the monopolistic nature of minimum commissions to the Restrictive Practices Court established by a Conservative government in 1956 under the Restrictive Trade Practices Act.

The Stock Exchange, taking the best legal advice, determined to defend itself. The organisation of its defence (as of the case against it) was a matter which, as soon became apparent, was likely to take years rather than months, since the principles at issue were hardly clear-cut, and the detailed evidence was a jungle. The Stock Exchange's preparations allegedly absorbed costs of some £3m and involved tens of thousands of pages of documentation: how much the OFT spent is not publicly known. In the end the date for a court hearing was fixed for January 1984. Had the Stock Exchange, which has been fairly criticised for reluctance at this time to adapt to a changing world, been able to take a more far-sighted view and anticipate an inevitable result, much trouble and expense could have been saved. However, its lack of adaptability in the 1970s eventually turned out for the best, by stimulating the Conservative government of the 1980s to push through radical new measures for the City, with repercussions far wider than the area of the Stock Exchange itself.

A Climate Favourable to Change

The impending court case was not the only catalyst for reform. There were other factors, both general and particular. In general after observation of New York's de-regulatory experience in 1975, there developed in London a reluctant but growing awareness of the inevitability of change. Ironically, however, this realisation was stultified by the impending court proceedings: the process of reform was frozen because of legal advice that in making any substantial modification of its Rule Book the Stock Exchange would be seen to recognise the validity of the case against it, which would undermine its defence. There was thus a virtual deadlock at the Stock Exchange from 1978 till 1983, though that was a time of major development elsewhere. This was a main reason why, when movement did become possible in 1983, it had the appearance of being rushed.

Actually, one progressive step was taken despite the deadlock: it related to the basic matter of membership of the Stock Exchange. Until 1969, membership had been essentially personal, in the sense that member firms were confined to partnerships of individual members, who had passed the Stock Exchange's qualifying tests. Large corporate entities were thus ineligible. However, in a market increasingly dominated by institutional investors the system had begun to creak: the jobbers needed a larger capital base (and went for mutual mergers in order to secure it), while the brokers began to have problems of cash flow. Accordingly in 1969 the Council of the Stock Exchange had amended its Rules, to permit any member firm, whether broker or jobber, to sell up to 10% of its equity to any one outsider — and, by extension, similar *tranches* of up to 10% each to a number of other outside buyers. Only in theory, however, did this open the door to wider participation: in practice, large outsiders like banks proved to be uninterested in acquiring such insignificant slices of investment. Accordingly, in 1982, the Stock Exchange felt it could without prejudice open the door further, and raised the ceiling for a single outsider's purchase from 10% to 29.9% (just short of the 30% level regarded by the Takeover Panel as a criterion of 'effective control'). Later in 1982 an American bank, Security Pacific, duly acquired 29.9% of the stockbroking firm of Hoare Govett.

Meanwhile, in July 1981, a strong reminder that reform was in the air had already been made apparent. After two minor but noisy crashes in the City, notably the collapse of Norton Warburg, the Department of Trade and Industry (DTI) had commissioned an eminent legal authority, Professor L.C.B. Gower, to report in depth on the whole matter of 'investor protection'. This subject, which is central to many of the reforms that have since taken place, was of prime concern to a Conservative government bent on greatly enlarging the number of private investors, both in existing stocks and in those due to be created by the programme of privatisation. Professor Gower's investigation was meticulous and his final report, which laid the foundation for the Government's White Paper on Financial Services, was not ready till 1984. It recommended a comprehensive overhaul of Britain's investor protection legislation and the establishment of a self-standing authority as the system's watchdog. He advised that to have the best chance of success in the intricate world of financial operations this should not be integrated into the judicial system of the country but should be City practitioner-based.

By this time the tendency towards change could not be mistaken even by the most conservative elements in the City. One factor, increasingly visible during a decade or more, was the notable growth of the worldwide short-term money markets, and of the Eurodollar market in which London had obtained and held a predominant position. Their emergence represented a quiet and unheralded revolution, on a scale comparable with the subsequent Big Bang, but its statistics were unreported, and its trading, sometimes called the 'Parallel Market', was in administrative terms virtually ignored by the Bank of England. However its economic impact, including the creation of new forms of life such as money brokers, could not be ignored by the

City at large. Nor could its technological apparatus, with the facilitation of telephoned and computerised dealing, both inter-bank in London (a striking new development) and international. With this there emerged anomalies formerly unthinkable, such as higher pay for assertive young dealers (the 'high wire men') than for the directors employing them. By the early 1980s these phenomena were becoming commonplace, and they facilitated the tendency towards innovations in the more staid and less adventurous world of the long-term market in equity capital and debt.

Even in the Stock Exchange there was by now a pessimistic yet salutary sense of eclipse. The high level of trading in New York in American Depository Receipts (ADRs), i.e. UK shares bought and sold over there with negotiated commissions and without stamp duty, began to be recognised as ominous. Altogether, if ever there was a moment when radical reform of the Stock Exchange seemed not merely urgently necessary but actually possible, it was in the early 1980s.

The Parkinson/Goodison Settlement, 1983

By 1983, a sufficiently realistic and conciliatory mood had developed on both sides for the possibility of an out of court settlement of the Restrictive Practices case to be seriously considered. Tentative discussions accordingly took place in the spring between the Bank of England, the Stock Exchange and the DTI under its then Secretary of State, Lord Cockfield, to see if the judicial hearing could be averted. However, as it turned out, with a General Election impending, no progress was then possible in a matter so complex and so sensitive politically. As soon as the Conservatives had been returned to office in June 1983 the matter was reopened, whereupon, in July, a settlement was quickly reached between the Chairman of the Stock Exchange, Sir Nicholas Goodison, and the new Secretary of State, Cecil Parkinson.

The nub of it was that the Government would drop the case on condition that the Stock Exchange consented to abolish the system of minimum commissions by the end of 1986. At the time, this agreement attracted rather limited attention: outsiders supposed it was an unimportant technicality, while some with more knowledge felt that it failed to curtail a more obvious restrictive practice, the broker/jobber distinction or 'single capacity' (dealt with below). There was even a tendency to see the deal as a sell-out by the Government. In fact it was a momentous step, which soon split wide open the old structure of the Stock Exchange. By early 1984, its implications were beginning to be apparent: by early 1985, after the Government's White Paper, the way ahead to Big Bang, and thence to a whole series of unpredicted consequences was unmistakable.

It is ironical that such large results should have flowed from such small beginnings. Admittedly fixed commissions were hallowed by tradition in London (at least, they had been established by Stock Exchange Rules of 1912, though in other sectors such as the discount market negotiated commissions were well understood), but in foreign eyes they were both unusual and unnecessary. This last point was later a cause for some pusillanimous anxiety in London, in case foreign brokers, accustomed to the mysteries of negotiated commissions, should, on admission to the Stock Exchange, prove to have a competitive edge over their less flexible British counterparts.

On the British Government side, there seems to have been a twofold motive in willingly avoiding court proceedings. On the one hand, of course, they might lose the case, though they rather doubted this. On the other, even if they won it there was a risk of an awkward outcome: the Restrictive Practices Court certainly had powers to make a judgment that would curtail the Stock Exchange 's operations, but it altogether lacked powers to create new capacities. Accordingly if the gilt-edged market in Government securities, in a monopolistic sense the most restricted sector of the Exchange, were effectively frozen as a result of the case, because its mode of broking and dealing was deemed illegal, the impact on the Government's liquidity, always largely dependent on the ready and continual sale of gilts, could have been immediate and serious. This embarrassing consequence was precluded by the settlement.

However, there were more constructive reasons why a Government re-elected in 1983 with a renewed mandate for reform should strongly favour any step tending to modernise the Stock Exchange. One such reason was investor protection — the keynote of which was to protect not just the two million existing investors in Britain but also the many more whom future privatisation should tempt to become shareholders and capitalists. Another reason was a widespread feeling, not disguised in New York and Tokyo, that our Stock Exchange had become stagnant, complacent and introverted, and would need drastic restructuring if it was ever to become internationally competitive again. (The Government had noted with disquiet that even the Euromarket in London, though obviously flourishing, was in fact dominated by foreign firms, mainly American). The threat was currently American, and potentially Japanese, rather than European: there seemed little to fear from stock exchanges on the continent. Amsterdam, though efficient, lacked a large domestic base. In other European countries rigidly regulated exchanges were geared to serve industry or to finance governments: the concept of a free-wheeling financial services centre functioning as an independent unit on the British pattern was unfamiliar in Europe. It followed that the London exchange, if only it could be made more efficient, would have very strong inherent advantages in Europe, and might well stand up to American and Japanese competition.

It was the Government's rather than the City's awareness of these shortcomings that supplied the motivation for the thoroughgoing reforms that took shape in the period 1983-87. Not that any individual in Westminster, Whitehall or the City foresaw the exact course events would follow. That course was in large measure mechanistic; one change triggered another. The abolition of minimum commissions would obviously have certain consequences: each firm would be free to set its own charges, which might be expected to vary according to the services rendered, or according to the size and importance of the client. However, soon after abolition was agreed it began to be clear that other less obvious adjustments, of far wider significance, would be necessary — or could be imposed.

Five of these main consequences can be conveniently identified. Directly or indirectly flowing one from another, they illustrate how what was at first lightly described as a Big Bang about stockbrokers' commissions grew into a real explosion, or series of explosions, of revolutionary scale. In one institution, the Stock Exchange, an ancient and famous face-to-face market on an historic trading floor would virtually disappear, leaving its startled bureaucracy to supervise a brand new system of distributed dealing and computer-driven disclosure. In the process, every other financial institution in London would be jolted into new awareness, new opportunity and new risk.

Consequences of the Settlement

Consequence One: Single to Dual Capacity

'Single capacity', which has already been mentioned, now no longer exists, so requires a brief explanation. It meant mandatory separation between the functions of the stockbroker and the stockjobber. The broker had to act exclusively as the client's agent, both in carrying out his instructions and in providing necessary advice and other services. He was expected to shop around for the best available bargain in the sale or purchase of stocks, and he lived by the percentage-based commission on the deal, which he levied on a fixed scale. The jobber, on the other hand, was not an agent, but an independent principal, a wholesaler, a market-maker, physically occupying a 'pitch' on the floor of the Stock Exchange, where he specialised in a number of stocks in competition with other jobbers. He lived by what was called the 'jobber's turn', namely the difference between the buying and selling price of what he traded. The client had to go to a broker, and in his turn the broker had to go to a jobber, to deal on his client's behalf. The system had undoubted integrity, but it was undoubtedly a cartel.

However, this 'singleness' of capacity protected the client: for example it ensured that the broker was not doubling as a market-maker, who might cynically trade in such a manner as to influence the price of a stock to his own profit while pretending to buy or sell at the best price for his client. As against this protection, the client suffered two disadvantages. First, he had little choice as to how much 'service' he wanted of his broker, in advice or research, but he had to pay the same fee anyway. Second, the commission did not always proportionately reflect the underlying cost of the transaction: a £100,000 deal might well involve no more work than a £1,000 one. Single capacity was therefore in effect a restrictive practice.

The Government was not expecting nor particularly desiring the abolition of single capacity when the Parkinson/Goodison deal on minimum commissions was made in 1983. However it quickly became apparent that guaranteed commissions were a prop that underpinned single capacity — or, in another sense, were a compensation that reconciled brokers to the prohibition against dual capacity. When minimum commissions went, single capacity was doomed. Doomed, that is, as a mandatory practice: some broking firms aimed to continue on a purely agency basis with personal clients, and have successfully done so. However the common response of brokers, on hearing that minimum commissions were to end, was to insist to the Stock Exchange Council that they could not survive unless permitted to be market-makers, in other words to join the cartel of the few remaining jobbing firms. The matching corollary, soon established subject to two safeguards mentioned below, was that jobbers should be permitted to broke; it was a licence to merge, and it would take effect in 1986.

The Stock Exchange decided that this important innovation would have to be subject to two new rules, to protect clients. The first would forbid a broker to deal with an in-house jobber, or market-maker, unless the latter demonstrably matched the best price then available. The second, which was related, would require a market-maker to advertise his pricing by continuous display over an electronic price service.

Though the ending of single capacity, when decided upon, was timed to coincide with the ending of minimum commissions in October 1986, a significant intermediate step was actually taken much earlier. From July 1984 member firms of the Stock Exchange, essentially when trading in foreign equities, were permitted to do so both in dual capacity and with negotiated commissions. This important adjustment might reasonably be called the *'first Little Bang'*. Other such preliminary portents were to follow: each of the five major consequences of the Parkinson/Goodison deal now being listed carried with it a relatively minor but anticipatory sub-consequence. The cumulative implications of these five 'Little Bangs' were immense. When the so-called Big Bang came in October 1986 the way had been so irrevocably prepared that it was more of an anticlimax than an explosion.

Consequence Two: The Move Upstairs

The requirement for the market-maker to protect the client's interests by continuous electronic price display was not in technical terms a total innovation. There already existed, for Stock Exchange members, a relatively primitive low-cost computer-and-colour-video information distribution network called TOPIC, and a database called EPIC. Moreover in the United States a sophisticated system, in effect an independent and dispersed exchange, called the National Association of Securities Dealers' Automated Quotations (NASDAQ), was already in operation. What was new, for London, was the drastic organisational implication of the latest technology. Few realised it at once, and not many even in October 1986, but when the Stock Exchange decided to instal SEAQ (Stock Exchange Automated Quotations), a system that broadcast all prices in all stocks to all member firms, it precipitated the end of an era. The traditional 'floor' was doomed to be first supplemented, then swiftly superseded by a 'move upstairs' (as it is called); this was away from the dealing floor to a 'distributed market', where market-makers in their own scattered premises can compete not face to face but by computer screen and, for the present at least, by telephone.

A distributed market only becomes feasible if all the participants have simultaneous access to identical information, which television and computer terminals can supply. What was in doubt, among London practitioners, was not the technical feasibility but the will to adapt. When the Stock Exchange's Strategic Planning Group reported to its Council in July 1984 in favour of developing SEAQ on the lines of the American NASDAQ, the proposal was agreed, but it was generally felt that the traditional mode of dealing would survive for years, precisely as the New York floor had done since 1975, and that SEAQ would initially be an adjunct rather than a successor to it. The implementation of SEAQ was timed, like other changes, to occur in October 1986, which left barely two years for the hectic development of that system and of all the supporting arrangements. These are outlined in later sections, which place the new technology in perspective.

However, as early as June 1985, well before Big Bang, a significant anticipatory step was taken, with the introduction of SEAQ International. This, though deployed in a geographically different field, served as a useful pathfinder for SEAQ. The system was at first experimental and technically rather unsophisticated by subsequent standards: but it was of value to members of the Stock Exchange who wanted a speeding-up of existing access into familiar areas for British investors, such as Australian and South African equities. How its screen quotations became technically more advanced will be touched upon later: in the present context it is enough to say that the inception of SEAQ International was for London a breakthrough, and amounted to a *'second Little Bang'*.

Consequence Three: Increased Corporate Membership

The third consequence of the Parkinson/Goodison settlement, like the previous two, followed in a logical, almost linear, progression. In summary, when brokers saw the end to minimum commissions coming, many, with an eye to self-preservation, calculated that single capacity must end also. In order to compete internationally they would need, if possible, to merge with jobbers, who alone had market-making expertise: at the same time, with a distributed market, they were about to face the need to acquire a daunting quantity of costly technological equipment, and the related overheads of staff and premises. All this required more capital than they possessed, and pointed to the abandonment of traditional partnerships in favour of limited liability, in corporate groups with international outlets. Hence from 1984, there was a sudden rush by many leading Stock Exchange members into corporate ownership by major British and foreign banks and conglomerates. It was an extraordinary episode, smacking in some cases of haste, panic or greed, occasionally with more regard to the compensation of senior partners than to the career expectations of their juniors. However, it was understandable, and against the fevered and brazen background of City events it attracted very little public attention.

The process was not of course universal: many firms of brokers, not exclusively in the provinces, preferred to retain their private client business, their partnerships and their independence. However the formerly insuperable barriers to entry from outside were bound to come down, and the transformation of what had been an exclusive club of individuals into a profession thrown open to the world's corporate membership quickly became an accomplished fact, despite some opposition grounded in the innate conservatism of individual Stock Exchange members, who found the new cosmopolitanism, linked in their view with an inescapable decline of ethical standards in the City, altogether lamentable and distasteful.

In fact, this particular writing had been on the wall for London ever since the transition to corporate membership in New York in 1970. By the early 1980s the de-regulatory tide was flowing strongly throughout the developed capitalist world. In this context de-regulation includes the lowering of barriers to market entry, the ending of monopolistic specialisations in financial markets, and the removal of exchange controls. In one sense it is an effect of facilitated capital movement as international controls are eased; in another, an effect of the technological contribution to the enhanced mobility of money. This technical factor, one of the staggering manifestations of our time, making obsolete all previous concepts of speed, accuracy and scale, can scarcely be exaggerated, whether applied to the movement of data or the mechanics of dealing. It was a cogent element among the various pressures leading inexorably to corporate membership of the Stock Exchange.

By June 1984 the Stock Exchange Council had formally conceded that barriers to corporate membership should in due course be removed. By June 1985 the principle of 100% outsider ownership of member firms had been accepted: however, at the same time a proposal to phase out individual membership completely, together with some other constitutional reforms, fell just short of the 75% vote needed for implementation. It seems to have been frustrated by a backlash from smaller firms and some junior members of larger ones. These resented what they felt were excessively generous takeover terms that many partners in leading firms were known to be accepting from outside buyers, during the prevailing wave of acquisitions, mostly at remarkably high prices. Their resentment showed itself in a reluctance to co-operate in wholly dismantling the traditional pattern of membership; but this was no more than a delaying tactic.

As already noted, partial outsider purchase of Stock Exchange member firms had long been permitted, up to a ceiling of 10% since 1969, and 29.9% since 1982. In a further step on 1 March

1986, a 'third Little Bang', the permitted proportion was raised to 100%, and simultaneously outsiders were permitted to apply for independent membership. Since this step was not sudden, but long forecast, and since provisional purchase arrangements had in several cases been concluded well in advance, the event attracted surprisingly little public attention; however it was a significant link in the causal chain between the Parkinson/Goodison deal of July 1983 and the Big Bang of October 1986. By late summer 1986 all the leading jobbing firms had been bought, as well as virtually every broking firm doing large-scale business with institutional investors. About 35 of London's 90 broking firms had entered, or begun to negotiate, mergers; nearly all those that had not, with the striking exception of Cazenove, were relatively small. (For selective lists illustrating the new wave of acquisitions, see Appendix A.)

It is impossible to estimate accurately how much the purchasers paid, and some of it was in shares not cash, but this whole exercise of corporate invasion, including the expense of capitalising newly acquired subsidiaries, certainly exceeded £1bn. And yet, to put this large-seeming figure into international perspective, it amounted to less than half the market capitalisation of a single major American investment firm, Merrill Lynch. As Plender and Wallace say in their book *The Square Mile*, this illustrates 'the uphill task that British securities firms faced under their new, and in many cases cosmopolitan, owners'. Merrill Lynch offers a highly relevant comparison because it took advantage of the de-regulatory provision of March 1986 which permitted outsiders to take up wholly independent membership of the Stock Exchange: so did another foreign giant, Nomura. The capital valuation of each of these two firms utterly dwarfed that of any possible British competitors in the field, and provokes one of the ominous and still unanswerable questions of the longer term.

Consequence Four: Reform of the Gilt-Edged Market

In one sense the drastic overhaul in 1986 of the ossified arrangements under which the gilt-edged market had been operating was another logical consequence of all that had happened since 1983. If restrictive practices were to be reformed, no part of the Stock Exchange was more restrictive than gilts. If broker/jobber separation was to give way to dual capacity, a resounding shake-up could be expected in that market, with its distorted near-monopoly by a few firms. If highly capitalised outsiders were to be admitted to Stock Exchange membership, they would predictably be attracted by the great scale of dealings in government stocks — at least so long as a reasonably strong pound ensured stability — and bring business.

In another sense, however, special factors in the gilts market — its size, and the great leverage in it of the Bank of England as the issuer of gilts — made events there as much a cause as a by-product of reform elsewhere. The Bank's regulation of the market is dominant, protecting the interests of all investors and monitoring the financial standing and risk exposure of all participants. Governments cannot finance their activities by taxation alone: the gap between revenue and total required revenue is the Public Sector Borrowing Requirement (PSBR), the great bulk of which has to be raised by sale on the Stock Exchange of government stocks (in a wide range of over 100 varieties offering interest rates from 2% to 15½%). Such stocks — amounting to some £130bn-worth currently on issue, and turning over at £1bn worth a day — overwhelmingly outweigh other government issues such as National Savings, Premium Bonds or short-term Treasury Bills. The underpinning of the gilts market is of course its attractiveness to institutional investors, for whom its principal advantage is the immediate re-convertibility of gilts into cash when required, since gilts are safe fixed-interest stocks, redeemable on a predetermined date.

If the gilts market is vital to the Government, it is equally true that the Bank of England, as the Government's agency in the City, is vital to the Stock Exchange: the Bank is by far its leading single client, since the turnover in gilts exceeds that in equities. The Bank's influence on the Stock Exchange throughout the recent period of structural reform was therefore predominant, and the Bank must share with the Government — and with the more far-sighted members of the Stock Exchange — the credit for the relative success of the reforms imposed.

These involved the complete overhaul of the system. For two hundred years it had been handled by a 'Government Broker', appointed by the Chancellor of the Exchequer to deal exclusively with the firms of jobbers who constituted the gilts market. In fact, the Government Broker was invariably the senior partner of a single firm, Mullens & Co., latterly Mr Nigel Althaus, and the number of jobbers with whom he dealt had shrunk to only seven. Of these, two firms, Wedd Durlacher Mordaunt and Akroyd & Smithers, monopolised 80% of the dealings. The Bank now decided to take the Government Broker on board, to be henceforth one of its own officials, supervising the Bank's own dealing room. It also decided to open the market, subject to compliance with stringent provisions, to all applicants for the new function of Gilt-Edged Market-Maker (GEMM), combining the formerly separate broker and jobber capacities. When the National Association of Pension Funds, representing some of the most massive investors, made a plea for the retention of single capacity in gilts dealings, the influence of the Bank was conclusive in insisting on change.

Applications to become GEMMs were invited, with a deadline in May 1985, and a large number of firms showed interest. 31 applied, but 4 later withdrew, doubting if adequate returns were possible against such competition, and 27 were eventually licensed. Even this number appeared to most outsiders, and to the participants, uncomfortably large. Their capitalisation, some £700m, seemed excessive in view of the estimated level of net earnings, about £100m, that the total of jobbers and brokers in gilts had been making under the prevailing system. It appeared inconceivable that a gilts turnover of some £260bn in 1985 could grow fast enough by 1987 to provide adequate profit on the new GEMMs' greatly increased level of capital, capital which was moreover required by the Bank's rules to be used exclusively for gilt-edged dealing. Furthermore it was expected that the dealer's 'margin' (essentially, the former jobber's 'turn' plus the former broker's commission) would fall to about 0.125%, while simultaneously the Bank would insist on stringent and therefore costly standards of computer efficiency.

The fear was that only a few heavily capitalised firms, such as Merrill Lynch, would have the resources to be able to stand inevitable initial losses, and that they would eventually dominate the market. When the new system came into effect with Big Bang in October 1986, expectations of early collapse for many smaller GEMMs were widely held. (In fact, however, the ensuing months, with continuously bullish prices as a prime factor, belied these gloomy assessments, and only one or two firms backed away.) Meanwhile, shortly before Big Bang, an intermediate step was taken which can well be termed the *'fourth Little Bang'*. In July 1986 the market in 'Bulldogs', which are non-UK Government sovereign or supranational fixed-interest bonds traded in London, was opened to dual capacity dealing.

Consequence Five: The Financial Services Act 1986

The four consequences of the Parkinson/Goodison deal so far listed were structural, with a directly mechanical effect on the way the Stock Exchange worked. The fifth was quite different. It was a major piece of legislation. Both in original inspiration and eventual impact it related to a much wider field than the Stock Exchange, but it is logically considered here among the effects triggered by Stock Exchange reform, effects that turned a big into a bigger bang. The fact that its origins are to be sought in Professor Gower's researches and reports should not disqualify it from convenient inclusion here in the causal chain reflected in these direct and indirect 'consequences'.

The Financial Services Act (FSA) that was promulgated on 7 November 1986, just after Big Bang, was designed to provide a new regulatory apparatus for increasingly de-regulated conditions: it was part of a process to impose public accountability and exposure, in the interests of investor/depositor protection, on giant institutions which otherwise could have enjoyed and exploited an excessive if not dangerous degree of freedom. It fits naturally enough into the sequence of statutes such as the Banking Act 1979 and the Lloyd's Act 1982. However it represents a more radical step, a more sweeping departure from the informal mode of internal control that had traditionally characterised the City's self-administration. Necessary though it had become to legislate for vastly changed conditions, this step would not have been practical at that moment and to that extent, had it not been for the catalyst provided in 1983-86 by the painfully contrived structural reform of the Stock Exchange.

Any government set on imposing a bureaucratic system of oversight on investment business would have had to tread carefully to secure on the one side an adequate measure of investor protection, while avoiding, on the other, an apparatus so rigid as to hinder business or drive the markets abroad, an outcome not difficult to cause. It was perhaps fortunate that the government which after much debate and amendment brought the FSA to fruition had two tendencies. On the one hand it was radical enough to care deeply about protecting individual investors (in pursuance of wider share-ownership and the extension of capitalist sentiment). On the other hand it was conservative enough to defer (as the Labour opposition would not have done in its place) to the feeling of City practitioners that to be internationally competitive they must be left as far as possible to regulate themselves, and that the controls created by the FSA should not form part of the ponderous judicial system of the state.

As it was, the step was drastic enough. The FSA described itself as an Act:

> 'to regulate the carrying on of investment business ... insurance business and business carried on by friendly societies ... to make new provision with respect to the official listing of securities, offers of unlisted securities, takeover offers and insider dealing ... disclosure of information ... relating to fair trading, banking, companies and insurance ... reciprocity with other countries in respect of facilities for the provision of financial services;' [*etc*]

This formidable range of authority has hardly yet been tested. The regulatory structure through which the FSA will operate is still largely embryonic, and the task of paving the way for its implementation has taken much longer than its drafters expected. But the new law is a revolution in itself. It aspires to identify and to bring under reasonable control a multiplicity of novel factors, economic, practical and ethical. These spring from technological innovation, from the globalisation of markets, from the removal of many bulkheads which used to compartmentalise the City, and from the rising influence in recent years of institutions that formerly carried much less clout — such as building societies, life assurance, unit trusts and pension funds. The FSA is a total overhaul of the original statutory coverage of investment business, dating from 1939. In the 1930s, more than one Committee was set up by the government of the day to report on share dealing scandals and also on the growth of unit trusts. From their findings derived the Prevention of Fraud (Investments) Act (PFIA), passed in 1939 but delayed in implementation till 1944, making it an offence to deal in securities without a licence. The PFIA, and a consolidating Act of the same title in 1958, continue to supply the specific statutory control over investment business, and will do so until the FSA becomes fully operative at last, supposedly on 1 April 1988 if that date is to be believed.

In recognition of altered conditions, there was a move in the 1970s, under a Labour administration, to revise or replace the PFIA; in 1977 a consultative document proposed various measures to strengthen the oversight of investment institutions and extend it to advisers and consultants. This momentum stopped when Labour lost the 1979 election, but was resumed under a Conservative government in 1981 when certain licensed dealers in securities (including Norton Warburg) collapsed, causing losses to investors. The upshot (already referred to) was Professor Gower's appointment by the DTI to review investor protection. Though his main findings were long delayed, an interim report came out in 1982, and led in the next year to amendments of the statutory Regulations on the licensing of dealers, and on their conduct of business.

Until this stage there was general scepticism about the Government's readiness to go any further. However, such doubts were soon dispelled by two factors. One was the continuing smell of scandal in the City's insurance and commodities sectors, which was felt to be politically very damaging. The other was the Parkinson/Goodison deal, and growing awareness that it portended both an inrush of outsiders into the Stock Exchange's preserves and the emergence of a new apparition, the financial services conglomerate. The case for a watchdog statute, refined to meet the new circumstances and calculated to serve somehow both the investor's rights and the City's need to compete internationally, became politically overwhelming; it also chimed with Gower's principal recommendation, that there should be a new Investor Protection Act. In October 1984 the Government committed itself to proceed.

There were two divergent undercurrents, one being the Governments's perceived need to act in the interest of City credibility. The other was a very strong feeling among City practitioners that a rigidly authoritarian oversight body, such as the Securities and Exchange Commission (SEC) set up in New York as a consequence of the crash of 1929, was unacceptable.

The DTI's White Paper presented by Norman Tebbit in January 1985, with broad objectives such as efficiency, flexibility and competitiveness, catered for this divergence by following Gower's line, proposing a statute that was comprehensive but was 'based so far as possible on self-regulation subject to governmental surveillance'. The FSA would accordingly set up (originally) two practitioner-based bodies, one the Securities and Investments Board (SIB), the other something called the Marketing of Investments Board (MIB) with particular responsibility for life assurance and unit trusts. (An MIB Organising Committee (MIBOC) was duly formed, but it soon merged with the SIB.) The principle was of a clear legal framework (the FSA), within which market forces should be allowed to operate, forces which only self-regulatory bodies of professional practitioners would know how to handle.

The outcome was the Financial Services Bill of December 1985, which after being subjected to some 600 amendments emerged eleven months later as the FSA. The fact that it consists of 212 sections and 17 Schedules, and in one annotated edition fills some 300 pages, is a measure of its bulk and complexity, which is not surprising given its innovatory scope. Among many ways in which it differs from the PFIA of 1958 is its creation of the SIB, with powers that represent a compromise between statutory regulation and self-regulation. Likewise it is new in setting a wider interpretation of 'investment business', going well beyond dealing in securities; and in stipulating that investors' rights shall be protected not just by criminal and administrative sanctions of great severity but by recourse to civil remedies — a point of acute sensitivity in the City.

Part I of the FSA, 'Regulation of Investment Business', comprises more than half the volume of the Act, and creates a pattern of authority to replace that inherited by the PFIA. It defines the scope of investment business, prohibits the carrying on of such business without authorisation (or exemption), and makes provision for such authorisation. This is to be by way of the SIB (to which the Secretary of State can delegate powers) and the subsidiary Self-Regulating Organisations (SROs), the launching of which has in practice proved so difficult and protracted: see their provisional layout in Appendices B and C. Part I of the Act further defines the criteria of good business conduct, and the SIB's powers of intervention, and makes provision for a Financial Services Tribunal drawn from a panel divided between legally qualified members and members qualified by professional experience. It also provides for a publicly accessible register of information, and enables the Secretary of State (rather than the Restrictive Practices Court) to make decisions, with the advice of the OFT, if any question of restrictive practice by an SRO should arise.

The rest of the FSA, Parts II to X, covers a wide field. It adapts the foregoing structure of authority to parts of the insurance industry (life assurance marketing and pension fund management), and to friendly societies. It specifies the criteria for the listing of securities, and for the offering of unlisted securities. It brings aspects of takeover offers (notably, increased protection of dissentient shareholders against compulsory acquisition) under the FSA rather than under the Companies Act 1985. It extends the coverage of the existing law on insider dealing. It makes rules governing what is permissible in the disclosure of information obtained under the Act. Among other provisions, it gives the Secretary of State a mechanism for acting internationally in British interests, e.g. in disqualifying foreigners from carrying on 'investment, insurance or banking business' in the UK if their country prevents British firms from operating there on comparably favourable terms. (In the spring of 1987 there were unconvincing suggestions that these sanctions might be used against Japan.)

Although the outline regulatory structure is set out in Appendices B and C, and the FSA was very much a part of the Big Bang climax of late 1986, most of the Act is still inoperative. Not till well into 1988, when the apparatus of SROs etc may at last be complete, with effective membership lists and with Rule Books checked by the OFT and approved by the SIB, will the FSA be tested. That there are strong and widespread doubts about its effectiveness reflects both the ingrained scepticism of the City and the unprecedentedly sweeping application of the FSA, which is symptomatic of the Bigger Bang to which the post-1986 City is tending.

All this illustrates how illusory it is to speak of Big Bang as a single conclusive event, whereas it is an upheaval taking several years. Attached to each of the consequences of the Parkinson/ Goodison accord that have been listed, one small but significant preliminary explosion has been noted. In this fifth and final consequence, a *'fifth Little Bang'* (though not chronologically the fifth) stands out. This was the establishment on 7 June 1985 of the Securities and Investments Board Ltd. It owed its genesis to the White Paper of the previous January, and to a decision in March by the DTI to support the idea of the SIB and to start it up in embryo, enabling it to recruit sufficiently good staff, at private sector rates, and to formulate its own basic rules well ahead of the parliamentary legislation which would provide its statutory functions.

Part Three : The Implications

Uncharted Territory

Part Two of this study covered the sudden changes that struck the City in 1983-86, many of them directly or indirectly stemming from the Parkinson/Goodison deal. Now Part Three will look at some of the further implications of these new developments, particularly as they dawned on members or would-be members of the Stock Exchange. Though the run-up to Big Bang in October 1986 can now be viewed in retrospect, and some events now even look obvious or inevitable, it all seemed a highly experimental and totally uncertain process at the time.

For various reasons, including generally bullish markets, most of the year since Big Bang has been a period of some stability and consolidation, but acute uncertainties must attach to any further forecasts. It is unprofitable to speculate in any detail about the shape of things to come, though it will not be difficult to close with a summary of some causes of doubt and uncertainty. Meanwhile it is instructive to look back at what the prospect seemed to offer, at the time when the reforms that are now established facts were still unfolding. In some regards expectations were to be fulfilled, in others not.

Lessons from the Experience of New York

As the five consequences of the Parkinson/Goodison settlement, as listed in Part Two, began to come into view in 1983-84, and as the pattern of the imminent future took shape, there was widespread misgiving in London. This extended from members of the Stock Exchange, who were most obviously at risk, to almost everyone connected with financial services. It was clear that an unprecented shake-up was unavoidable: it was bound, at best, to be destabilising, while at worst it might lead to a general foreign takeover by giant Japanese and American conglomerates, and the collapse of many established firms. Opinion was very divided as to what to expect, but the most thoughtfully reasoned assessments were based on the experience of New York since 1970. This had a strong influence on major City brokers with an institutional clientele. Judging by what they had seen happening at the NYSE, many of them decided (rightly) that they could sell their partnerships at very high prices to large firms, and (wrongly) that despite technological advance the famous floor of the Stock Exchange would long be preserved as the focus of dealing.

De-regulation had been imposed in New York not in one stage but in two, and this softened its impact. First there had been the decision to permit corporate ownership of NYSE firms from 26 March 1970; second, the abolition of fixed commissions on 1 May 1975, an exercise known as 'Mayday'. In between, though competition in commissions was still prohibited, a form of concealed competition was widespread, both by way of discounts offered to the client, and by way of services such as research and investment advice. The question pondered by New York firms before Mayday in 1975 was, would large institutional clients be attracted by cheaper commissions, or be ready to pay as much, or more, for old-fashioned services and high-quality research? In the event, neither option predominated: what emerged was the major clients' conspicuous preference for brokers with sufficient resources to offer both a steeply reduced commission *and* first class services.

As for commissions, these fell further than anyone had expected. Shortly before 1 May 1975 a price-lead was set by Goldman Sachs with a reduction of 8% on the rates of fixed commissions charged to institutional clients. However the average institutional rates charged by NYSE members quickly dropped far lower and by 31 May were 25% down, and still dropping. By 1977 they were 40% down, and further falls in 1983-85 reduced them substantially further.

When, against this pared-down scale of commissions, was set their clients' exacting expectations in services and research, the competition proved more intense than many small firms, even ones long known for their high standing, could sustain. Admittedly some of the more conservative New York firms, whether because they had become under-capitalised or technologically uncompetitive, were by April 1975 already going under, as victims of the market depression occasioned by the final throes of the Vietnamese war. But this process was accelerated by the de-regulation of Mayday, and a large number of mergers resulted. One example was Baker Weeks, which had had a reputation for its research: it was acquired by the broking firm Reynolds Securities, which was later taken over by Dean Witter, itself subsequently acquired by the department store chain Sears Roebuck. One particularly large firm, Shearson Lehman, itself a subsidiary of American Express, was a merger of at least thirty smaller brokers.

However, it would be misleading to imply that Mayday led merely to a narrowing-down of the NYSE to a few conglomerates resembling each other in the giant scale and compendious range of their operations. If anything, the variety of type actually increased. At one end of the spread were shoestring 'discount brokers', such as Quick & Reilly, said to operate on such a starkly economical basis, offering minimal services, that they could afford to undercut the most expensive firms' commissions by some 70%. At the aristocratic end of the scale a few firms, such as Smith Barney, still survived, providing services to match their reputation.

Other categories on the varied post-Mayday scene were major wholesale-dealing investment banks like Morgan Stanley, as well as national retailing companies, 'wire houses', such as A.G. Edwards. Niches had also developed in specialisations: for instance there were firms which did not themselves trade or broke, but were contracted to fulfil the 'back office' services, that is the clearing and settlement functions, for other NYSE firms' trading. A few small dealers, too, operated on a 'boutique' scale.

If all this amounted to a distinctly patchy picture, for British broking and jobbing partnerships in 1983-84 trying to read the omens for themselves in New York's experience there was a compensating factor. The overall volume of trading on the NYSE, presumably stimulated by cheaper commissions, rose steeply after 1975. In the next ten years the number of people employed by the NYSE doubled, and this evidently represented prosperity, since the price of a seat, after falling in 1975-78 to $50,000, recovered to $500,000 by 1985.

It is difficult, without an excess of detail, to apportion comparative gain and loss in the New York scene in the period 1975-85. However, it was apparent that there were many losers, notably the small firms already mentioned, and others that failed to find a special type of business in which to survive. Another category doing worse since 1975 had been small private investors, who, lacking the bargaining muscle of large institutional clients, and often needing a broker's personal service, had commonly had to pay more for it, not less. Consequently they had tended to trade less — or if they were as active as before, it had been through a greater use of institutionalised intermediaries such as retirement schemes or 'mutual funds' (unit trusts in Britain).

This last possibility was not necessarily a bad thing, given the common political objective of both the US Administration and the present British Government to encourage the increased popularisation of share ownership, and given the fact that intermediaries offer a means to this. However, from the British standpoint in the mid-1980s, looking to New York for indications of what to expect, the lesson was clear: small brokers were vulnerable to being squeezed out, and the individual private investor might expect a harder deal than before. One corollary was equally plain: the small British broker, particularly in the provinces, might well expect to retain his individual clientele, especially if services were kept up and commissions were kept down. (In Britain these expectations have been largely fulfilled.)

Another corollary was also evident. If there were losers there were gainers too. Most conspicuous were the large investment firms, which since 1975 had grown larger and more dominant. For them, trading was now cheaper, so they traded more. Institutional trade had expanded to some 75% in volume of all NYSE dealing. 'Block trades' (i.e. transactions involving at least 10,000 shares) as a proportion of overall volume had risen from about 15% in 1975 to about 50% in 1985. Some of the larger firms by now had almost the configuration of a supermarket: in Sears Roebuck shoppers could buy real property, insurance or shares as well as the regular stock-in-trade of a department store. However, this 'one-stop shopping' was said to be proving an expensive service to provide, and some firms had over-extended themselves in it. Annual pre-tax profits in this field were calculated to have fallen steeply from about 11% in 1980 to nearer 6% in 1985.

Indeed by the mid-1980s the largest profits in New York, approaching 15% pre-tax, were being made by big investment banks: their most rewarding areas were proving to be not traditional broking but operations associated in Britain with merchant banking, such as mergers, arbitrage and the underwriting of initial public offerings. Many new techniques had emerged, such as the packaging of loan assets, e.g. mortgages and car loans, into securities saleable to investors. In addition, American firms were increasingly going in for risk-taking on their own account, as in 'over-the-counter' trading in securities, and the arrangement of sophisticated options programmes. Above all, the emerging trend was towards trading in 'debt', which might constitute 20% of the business of a typical major firm.

This competitive diversification, as much as the de-regulation which had encouraged it, had the result of reducing commissions as a proportion of gross revenue of NYSE firms, from about 50% in 1975 to about 20%. Conspicuous among New York firms operating in the diversified field were the traditional 'special bracket' names (Salomon Brothers, Goldman Sachs, First Boston, Merrill Lynch and Morgan Stanley) together with

Shearson Lehman. Given their huge capitalisation, it was hard to imagine them not establishing in due course, together with the Japanese in particular, a similar grip on financial institutions in London, beginning with the Stock Exchange.

The Prospect for British Brokers and Jobbers, 1983-86

Though the repercussions of Big Bang would eventually have an impact on all Britain's financial institutions (indeed they began to be felt long before October 1986, as coming events cast their shadow before, and corporate strategies were recalculated), the people most centrally and immediately affected were stockbrokers and stockjobbers. From 1983 on, with a mounting sense of urgency, they were forced to estimate, from observation of past experience at the predominantly domestic market in New York and from their judgment of future international trends relevant to London, what course of action would be in their and their firms' best interests.

It was an extremely difficult choice, and in retrospect they deserve credit for the orderly way in which they took it, though, to be sure, for some the bitter pill of selling out was sweetened by the unexpectedly high prices banks proved willing to pay for their businesses. For instance £100m was paid by the Hong Kong & Shanghai Bank for the acquisition of the broker James Capel, and £200m by Barclays to form its conglomerate with a jobber (Wedd Durlacher Mordaunt) and a broker (de Zoete & Bevan). Such sums were spent to acquire not the physical assets, which were worth much less, but the intangible reputation of the firms acquired and the expertise of their staff.

Typically, the London-based broker or jobber faced six obvious courses, not all mutually exclusive:

(1) *To join a British conglomerate.* This would offer advantages in multiple trading outlets, in association with a fuller range of financial services, and in increased capital

backing. That last factor would be a valued reassurance in the event that lower commissions brought lower profits.

(2) *To go international,* joining a foreign firm. This had the attraction of distant outlets, but less attractively suggested exposure to unaccustomed risk business. British brokers, and even merchant bankers, though strong on agency and advisory work, had less experience of risk business, with its associated requirement of substantial venture capital, than their American counterparts.

(3) *To make a broker/jobber merger.* This would be logical under dual capacity but involved acceptance of substantial and ponderous statutory safeguards, including the apparatus of 'compliance', in order to ensure avoidance of any conflict of interest to the client's detriment.

(4) *To stay independent.* This was attractive to smaller London firms, as to the provincial ones, who were unlikely to be bid for by outsiders. In numerical terms about 200 out of 240 member firms elected to stay in their existing agency role, assuming a profit was still to be made from providing services to individual and minor institutional clients. (Two moderate-sized firms, E.F. Matthews and Dunkley Marshall, made minor history by combining before Big Bang as a new firm, J.T. Parrish, with shares listed on the Stock Exchange.)

(5) *To start a 'boutique'.* Some individual brokers, after accepting 'golden handcuffs' to join another firm for a limited period, planned to wait till the term was ended, in order to leave and start their own independent business, free of the disagreeable constraints of subordination in a conglomerate. (One such new firm is Ark Securities, with 16 founding partners, mainly from Quilter Goodison/Hong Kong & Shanghai, and a total staff of 40.)

(6) *To opt out.* Some senior brokers and jobbers retired early, utterly repelled by the prospect of increasingly depersonalised dealing on electronic channels, of relegation at a stroke from senior employer to faceless employee, and of longer hours and more intensive work. (The City's dealing hours have indeed changed drastically,

and a small social revolution is exemplified in the experience in 1986 of commuters from Haslemere, Surrey, deep in the 'stockbroker belt'. Finding their first fast train departure for London, 7.14 a.m., too late for early business, they persuaded British Rail to provide a new service at 6.42. Another revolution is eating habits: the extended City lunch is out of favour, while the 'working breakfast', till recently a barely credible concept, is now not uncommon.)

The View from Outside, 1983-86

If those were the options open to brokers and jobbers in a drastically changing world, the other side of the coin must be mentioned. This was the choice available to British and foreign outsiders as they contemplated the novel prospect of openings in what had always hitherto been a severely restricted area. In simple terms, the choice was to buy their way in or to stay outside. The decisions they reached were very varied.

There was a rush, already described, to buy up the larger City firms; and yet, not all those who might have been expected to join it did so. Only one leading Wall Street investment banker (Shearson Lehman, buying L. Messel) took steps to acquire a British stockbroker, and no Japanese firm at all did so. Indeed, of the ten largest London brokers that were taken over, only four were bought by foreigners.

If these facts suggest a relatively low level of overseas interest, it must be conceded that the Stock Exchange, though a market of such historic magnitude and status in City tradition, was no longer a giant in world terms compared with New York and Tokyo, and in 1983-86 did not strike all observers as exemplifying the urge to adapt to innovation. Its capacity to operate the new dealing technology remained to be demonstrated; its merger with the International Securities Regulatory Organisation (ISRO), destined to provide an internationally formidable organisation, had not yet occurred; like much of the City it was subject to strong political criticism from the Labour Party, and there was no certainty that the Conservatives would win the 1987 or 1988 general election, indeed for many months their chances looked poor. Of much more immediate interest to American investment banks, to judge from the distribution of their London personnel, was the great profitability of the Eurobond market, or the high return to be found in telephone trading with the Continent in international securities.

At least this lack of enthusiasm has resulted in overwhelming British strength being retained in the London equities market, which is a reassurance to those who expected Big Bang to signalise wholesale foreign takeover. Such fears were not irrational; foreign brokers were perceived to hold some strong cards. One was that they were known to be wholly accustomed to negotiated commissions and to dual capacity, which it was expected that they would manage at first more expertly than their British counterparts. But above all, the largest of them were so massively capitalised as to justify gloomy expectations that it was only a matter of time before the entire British stock market came into the grip of a few outside firms disposing of sufficient resources to undertake wholesale transactions (such as 'bought deals', the guarantee, purchase and resale of entire stock issues) of a kind familiar enough in the USA but virtually unknown in Britain.

However, if foreign interest in acquiring existing Stock Exchange firms was half-hearted, it was still sufficient, coupled with parallel interest among British firms (with Bank of England encouragement), and added to direct entry to the floor by the giants Merrill Lynch and Nomura, to transform the market. The process was notable both for the speed with which it happened and the sensational level of some of the prices paid. The acquirers guessed, ahead of the game, that single capacity was doomed, and the early efforts of some, notably Barclays and S.G. Warburg, to buy major broking and jobbing firms, served to accelerate the process that they were anticipating. They judged, furthermore, that advances in electronics had now made possible a quantum jump in the techniques of trading; the heavy capitalisation of the new conglomerates could now set the pace in the immensely costly acquisition of new equipment. They also perceived, in assessing potential business growth, that new factors had been created; for example, instantaneous transmission of market data had rendered provincial extensions of international trading economic to operate on a small scale, as in an investment boutique.

The scale and the timing of the rush of acquisitions that took place is sufficiently illustrated, although selectively, in Appendix A.

The Effusion of New Rules

One of the most conspicuous by-products of Big Bang was the mass of new regulations still a year later being hurriedly formulated to meet its requirements. This is confusing to an amateur outsider, daunting and costly to a professional practitioner, and potentially deterrent to a foreign investment banker as he ponders the case for entering the London market. Whether the City will sink under the weight of its own regulation, as pessimists predict, remains to be seen.

The general trend is not new. There had been at one time a very skeletal system of regulation, informally but effectually administered within a City where most of the leading figures knew each other well and came from closely similar social and economic backgrounds. This homogeneity was itself a real disciplinary sanction. However this close-knit pattern had been becoming, over the course of twenty-five years, more and more overlaid by a busier, more heterogeneous and much more impersonal way of City life, which in regulatory terms had to be increasingly formalised and elaborate.

There were many causes, including the rise of the Eurobond market, the entry to London of hundreds of foreign banks (with acute accompanying problems of supervision, split between the London 'host' authority and the foreign 'parent' bank), and a number of scandals, each tending to provoke a tightening of the rules after the event. However, it is paradoxical that current 'de-regulation' has critically accelerated the process of regulation: firms are permitted to expand greatly their range of operations, to do more kinds of work than ever before, but at the same time are compelled to disclose more information, to back their ventures with more capital, and to erect ever more stringent safeguards against foul play. This may be discouraging to the criminally-minded: it is certainly discouraging to the legitimate operator who in a less regulated environment could benefit from the use of his enterprise and innovation.

A principal objective of the new regulations is investor protection, stemming from considerations both of equity and, cynically enough, of politics. The investor has to be safeguarded against two contingencies, financial instability and deliberate malpractice. Whether the growing sophistication of technology makes it harder or easier for the dishonest dealer to defraud his client is a question that has been inconclusively argued. On the one hand, electronic communications facilitate surveillance and leave an instantaneous audit trail, less easily fudged than retrospective paper records. On the other, the computer cannot betray its operator's mind: it depersonalises what was formerly a fiduciary relationship between identifiable individuals. The crook will always be tempted to cut a corner, and will sometimes succeed. Also the application of more rules has the sad effect of creating more offences, and almost automatically more crooks — as demonstrated by the prohibition of insider dealing, attaching in recent years severe penalties to something that was previously considered legitimate.

One specific aim of the subsidiary regulations under the FSA is greater 'visibility of dealing'. Electronic systems now make it feasible for all contracts to be time-stamped in seconds, so that a precise moment is indelibly manifested on the print-out, coupled with a specification of the dealer's 'capacity' at that moment, whether as a 'principal' or as the client's 'agent': these facts, together with the price, are strong evidence relating to 'best execution', i.e. that the client was given the most advantageous deal then available. The prospect of section 62 of the FSA, providing for civil litigation by the client against the consultant or agent, is proving particularly contentious and unwelcome to professional practitioners.

A looser and wider aim of the FSA, not always attainable with the same precision, is to control as large a range of 'ethical' considerations as can in practice be covered by regulation. Under Chapter V of Part I (coupled with Schedule 8) of the Act the Secretary of State and the SIB (and by obvious delegation, the SROs) are empowered to make 'Conduct of Business Rules', the contravention of which becomes subject to various criminal or administrative sanctions. The potential scope of these rules, though elaborately defined, is very broad, and extends from the ordinary tenets of long accepted business procedures into areas where regulators must tread with wariness, such as the proprieties of advertising, the implications of gifts and entertainment between companies, the tiresome practice of 'cold-calling' by insurance salesmen, and the detailed criteria for providing 'best advice' for inexperienced clients or for drawing up agreements with them.

The Delicate Regulatory Balance

The imposition of this indigestible mass of new rules, and the provision for even more in 1988 when the SROs' Rule Books will surely at last be operative, cannot be attributed merely to bigoted politicians and bureaucratic civil servants. It has had the weight of the Bank of England's authority behind it: not the least interesting development of recent years has been the conversion of the Bank, belated in the view of many, from belief in the old informality of control which characterised its methods before the 'secondary banking crisis' of the 1970s, to support for the new structure of detailed and statutory oversight. The conversion is surprising: the mass of rules is very great, and questionably digestible: the outcome must be in doubt until it can be shown that a sufficiently wise and delicate regulatory balance has been achieved.

The need for a sensitive equilibrium can be simply expressed. If rules are too loose, or action to enforce them too feeble, they will not protect the public, and will fail in their main purpose. If rules however are too rigid they will infallibly obstruct the swift transaction of business and encourage it to move to somewhere less restrictive. Both these considerations are acutely relevant in the newly internationalised securities industry. The public's need of protection is greater than before, and 'best execution' requires to be incontrovertibly demonstrated: at the same time technology and the reduction of exchange controls have made the industry mobile to an extent that only a decade ago would have been unbelievable.

The problem of balance is the problem of combining a judicious minimum of essential oversight with a maximum of desirable self-regulation, so as neither to leave the investor over-exposed nor to cramp the professional's freedom of operation. The crowning irony of the close attention paid in the 1980s to the Stock Exchange (in terms of turnover, a relatively small part of the City's market structure) would be if the regulatory reforms that this engendered were to drive the most prosperous elements in that structure, such as the massive Eurobond market, out of London altogether, into a less controlled and more welcoming environment.

The attractions of London as an international financial market are obvious and often stated. Some are attributable to luck (such as the time-zone factor), some to inherited historical advantages (e.g. political stability and the priceless asset of the English language), others again to the City's accumulated professional expertise and tradition of integrity, still despite the erosion of recent years a benefit of great value. However no single factor is more important than the one which is unfortunately the most vulnerable of all, namely the relative liberty from intrusive control which has always till now characterised the City as a financial centre. The principal reason for the existence in London of flourishing Eurobond and foreign currency markets has been this freedom of operation, often favourably compared with the over-regulated condition of New York and other financial centres.

There are those who assert that this freedom was excessive and made inevitable some of the numerous institutional crashes and scandals of the past quarter-century; there are many who recognise that it had to be replaced by statutory controls, which has indeed happened in the past decade in the fields of banking, and of Lloyd's, and of financial institutions generally; but no one with practical knowledge can fail to see that the imposition of unduly burdensome controls must risk driving the market out. Its vulnerability and, in a computerised age, its total mobility, have political as well as economic implications. Britain's securities industry, expanded via banks and insurance into every kind of financial institution, is estimated to employ at least two million people. Anything threatening to undermine it is a major national risk, which must be recognised.

The SIB and its regulations were not, of course, created in a vacuum. In the Stock Exchange (which has an enviably good record of performance and integrity vis-a-vis its clients, and was unconnected with the critical Norton Warburg crash) there has existed for many years a sophisticated set of rules to protect the investor, including provision for compensation in the event of default. However, for reasons sufficiently explained in Part Two, the tight little club of the Stock Exchange was split apart in 1983-86, and opened to worldwide participation by outside firms. These included conglomerates to whom the City's methods were not familiar and even the correlation of 'word' and 'bond' was not automatically a first priority. The consequence was that the Stock Exchange's Rule Book (itself at the root of the initial dissatisfaction that led to Big Bang) become not just inadequate, but irrelevant to the wider membership of the newly de-regulated, physically dispersed and culturally heterogeneous structure.

The SIB is the new bureaucratic accretion on that structure. Whether it will work efficiently remains to be proved. What is certain is that it is generating an infinity of paper to maintain its oversight, and is creating many new procedures (such as the 'client agreement letter' giving a broker formal authority to act on a client's behalf).

In creating new procedures it is also creating new offences, and it has at its disposal formidable disciplinary powers. In these circumstances it is alarming to note, one year after Big Bang, how many individuals and small firms, subject to SIB oversight, have not yet grasped the exacting nature of the new system to which, when it is promulgated in 1988, they will be exposed. Many, not so much in stockbroking but on the consultant fringe of investment and insurance work, act as though unaware that failure to comply may land them in court or out of business.

Behind the dauntingly unfamiliar new apparatus of regulation many interlocking intentions can be perceived. One is to formalise with precise rules as many principles of business practice and ethics as possible, even if some of them are already stated in common or statute law. Another is to reassure investors, and political critics, by the sheer comprehensiveness of the rules. Another is to bring into being a completely new private policing system of 'compliance officers' — a concept borrowed from the USA — who are to check procedures within their firms and ensure that their colleagues recognise and fulfil them. Another, in the event of malpractice or corporate collapse, is to avoid the expense and delay of standard litigation by providing the investor with a reliable prospect of compensation, and an ultimate arbitrator in the shape of an ombudsman.

The SIB, as the most conspicuous instrument created by the FSA, is revolutionary in the scale of its implications. That is not to say that the FSA aspires to monopolise the regulation of the City: great areas of responsibility must continue to be subject to the administrative sanctions of the Bank of England or the DTI, and the less formalised pressures of the Monopolies Commission and the Takeover Panel — not to mention the underlying safety-net of the law of the land, including a wave of new legislation bearing on company and business practice. But the SIB, and all that goes with it, constitutes a massive additional burden on an already hard-worked system. There is serious risk of confusion between overlapping supervisory bodies, particularly where multi-functional firms are answerable to self-regulatory authorities. Among the priorities of the DTI in administering the FSA (which, though law for several months, has hardly begun to take effect through its still embryonic subsidiary legislation) is to determine how these authorities should be coordinated, and how for instance, one 'lead regulator' is to emerge when several share an interest in a firm or a transaction.

If rationalisation within Britain is going to be difficult of attainment, the difficulty of achieving logical and acceptable correlation of rules on an international basis challenges the imagination. However, to an extent which is hardly recognised outside the circle of professional practitioners, such correlation is already overdue and will soon become essential. Presumably it will come about in the end experimentally, piecemeal, with maximum untidiness and recrimination. Unfortunately, perception of a need commonly lags behind the need itself (which is why the City's financial revolution is occurring now and not five years ago), but the increasing fluidity of money and the new technological facilities behind the startling globalisation of business, will not wait. It will suddenly be found that some degree of international regulation can no longer be deferred.

When this happens, London is likely, as a result of Big Bang, to be in a much stronger position than before to influence the system. Evidence for this likelihood can already be seen: a global financial market already exists. This is clear from the operations of major New York investment firms such as Salomon Brothers, which are heavily expanding their staffs in London and Tokyo and creating a world-based triangular network. However, when it comes to international comparisons, American banks are gravely handicapped on their home base by the Glass-Steagall Act of 1933 (the Depression-induced law which structurally separated commercial banking from investment banking and which de-regulation in 1970 and 1975 did not sweep away). An ironic consequence of Glass-Steagall is that outward-looking American banks such as Citicorp cannot for instance underwrite securities at home, yet freely do so in London's relatively unrestricted Euromarket. London's superior environmental attractiveness to New York, so long as Glass-Steagall remains unrepealed, has been enhanced by Big Bang. Moreover, any comparison with Tokyo is equally favourable to London in this respect, since Tokyo's system is not yet de-regulated: deposit ceilings and fixed commissions are still applied there.

Hence, one of the medium-term implications of the City's revolution is that it enhances London's prospects as a global market. What is unfortunately less auspicious is that as soon as bear conditions return the sheer resources required to operate in strength on an international scale may price many British firms out of the market, and give the advantage to the heavily capitalised conglomerates from Japan and the USA. The biggest single factor in this ultimate competitive test is the cost of technology: there is a gleam of encouragement in the fact that unit price in electronics tends to fall with the passage of time.

The Timetable for Implementation

The process of cranking up the new regulatory engine from cold is proving extremely protracted and difficult. The price is now being paid for the virtual freeze on any change-oriented thinking at the Stock Exchange between 1978 and 1983 (a tactical position under the shadow of expected litigation, as already explained). However, progress is laboriously and systematically being made, and it must be admitted that, given the complex machinery being extensively rebuilt on new lines, and the need to educate a very sceptical and unconvinced body of practitioners in the new criteria of their professionalism, the long delay in getting it to work is no surprise.

The SIB is an anomalous body. It was essentially created to become the 'Designated Agency' in terms of section 114 of the FSA, that is, the 'body corporate ... able and willing to discharge all or any of the functions' which the Secretary of State at the DTI was empowered to delegate for the due regulation of the financial services. But in order to recruit its staff and prepare the ground for operating the functions which would be delegated to it, in time for the FSA becoming law in late 1986, the SIB needed to be set up well in advance. It is essentially a limited liability company paying its staff at private sector rates, a point on which its Chairman, Sir Kenneth Berrill, insisted in order to ensure he secured personnel of high quality. Schedule 9 of the FSA specifies that the SIB 'shall not be regarded as acting on behalf of the Crown, and its members ... shall not be regarded as Crown servants'. Nevertheless, it is a highly influential body, partly owing to the impressive quality of its senior staff, and partly because the Government is heavily and controversially committed to its success. No one was much surprised when Berrill of the SIB was allowed by the DTI to win a sharply argued dispute with Borrie of the OFT in mid-1987 about the potentially restrictive new principle of 'polarisation' in the rules for banks and insurance companies as to which firms they might or might not recommend to their clients.

A comment is called for here on polarisation, one of the odder concepts that have emerged in the post-Big Bang environment. Its purpose is investor protection, as the SIB would wish: its effect will also be undoubtedly restrictive, as the OFT has perceived. In essence, under SIB regulation, offices and individuals marketing or recommending services such as life assurance or unit trusts will have to make a declared and permanent choice — *either* to be seen to act as the direct representatives of a main firm, group or institution, and as such to offer a client the exclusive service or product of the organisation they serve, *or* to be separately and independently constituted, giving advice not in favour of a parent organisation's service but objectively across the board. This is an invidious choice. It strikes at the root of what many bank managers and insurance and investment advisers have felt to be their honourably conducted function, of recommending impartially their own firm's product or that of another firm, guided principally by the client's perceived need.

The SIB's defeat of the OFT in this regard has provoked the creation of a ginger-group, CAMIFA (Campaign for Independent Financial Advice) led by Sir Richard Powell and representing most of the leading life assurance companies. CAMIFA is outspokenly critical of three major clearing banks (Barclays, Lloyds and Midland) which have opted for the exclusive "company representative" choice. The SIB and DTI can expect to come under vigorous lobbying to reconsider their position on polarisation, and it is all too likely that further delays in implementing the rules will follow. As the long-deferred date for the full activation of the SROs and related apparatus goes on receding, and as disconcerting stories gather momentum regarding the unmanageable bulk and complexity of the new Rule Books, the SIB's never shining popularity has been further dimmed. It is seen as an implausible crossbreed, attempting severely but unconvincingly to fulfil two separate functions simultaneously, serving both the public and private sectors even where their interests are disparate.

This hybrid role for the SIB, as a private company set up to match the criteria of a new statute and to exercise oversight imposed by government action under the law, is a contentious one. To viewers on the political left, the SIB's impartiality is suspect, and the indications are that a Labour government would wish to turn it into a branch of the DTI, with recourse to the lawcourts for its sanctions. Among City practitioners, it has been viewed with a different sort of scepticism: is it feasible, the critics ask, for the SIB to be simultaneously arbiter and policeman and prosecutor? In face of these hostile viewpoints, it is altogether unfortunate that the SIB is not yet in working order. It has not escaped notice that recent investigations into City conduct have tended to be handled by the Bank of England or the Takeover Panel or the DTI or the Fraud Squad, largely because the SIB's gestation period as a functioning reality has been so protracted.

It is the chain of authorisation which has taken so long to forge since the FSA came on to the statute book in November 1986. Basically the Act allowed the Secretary of State to ask Parliament to let him delegate certain powers to the SIB; those powers included oversight over the SROs, with the right to investigate wrongdoing and if necessary to prosecute. The SROs would in turn be empowered to oversee and discipline their members on principles relating to fair practice and business efficiency. Those principles were to be cumulatively embodied in the Rule Books of the SIB and SROs, and those Rule Books (when sufficiently prepared, itself a long and controversial task) would then be subjected to the scrutiny of the DTI, through the medium of the OFT. It is not surprising that despite the obvious urgency, this process has been bogged down in consultation and argument, and the membership of some SROs is still far from completely established. New staff have had to undertake from scratch new work for which no precedent existed. Some of the criteria they have had to codify have been intangible, such as the 'benchmarks' or sets of minimum standards in business practice. Others have been quantitatively questionable, such as the required capital ratios, and investor compensation fund levels. As the various SRO Rule Books have at last been edited into shape and presented to the SIB for ratification, public attention, not least in the City, has been markedly irreverent, concentrating unkindly on the gross avoirdupois of these monumental compilations, and hinting that the likelihood of their being fully obeyed, or even read, is slight indeed.

When the SIB eventually becomes fully operative, it must be hoped that it will merit, and command, the general support it now lacks. It may then vindicate the high costs it is generating, which are at present widely seen as excessive. The overall budget for the new regulatory machinery, which falls on financial institutions rather than directly on the public, is in the range of £20m, including £6m for the SIB alone. This is of course not all new expenditure: it has always cost money to regulate the City, and it is much cheaper than the $100m budget of New York's long-established SEC. However, that only represents a small part of the extra cost to the City. Taking into account compliance officers and others required to implement the new arrangements, the annual cost, at present rates, of self-regulation in the City will be nearer £200m than £20m. Nevertheless even this figure is dwarfed by the expense of the new technology: that, far more than the apparatus of control, may prove to be what distinguishes the sufficiently capitalised from the rest, the future survivors from those who will be broken when bear markets return at last.

A Crash course in Technology

A section in Part Two of this study, entitled 'Consequence Two: The Move Upstairs', described the abrupt elevation of computers and TV screens from mere adjuncts of dealing (as they were) into the indispensable tool, if not main motor, of the system that they have become. They represent the technological imperative, the aspect of Big Bang that was least easy for non-experts to grasp, but that was also least capable of being hustled by management to fit a timetable. Its implementation has been, and continues to be, an extremely costly exercise. In 1984-86 a typical major securities firm would have invested some £30m on a totally new electronic system, without which after 27 October 1986 it would neither be able to make a market competitively nor settle the formalities of its deals at all. That investment would not be a definitive or limited one. Attached to it would be two main requirements, one for extensive dealing-floor space worth some £50 a square foot, and the other for staff able to handle the equipment. Over it would loom the further prospect of replacing most of the electronic hardware when its efficient life of some four years would end; and the ever-present prospect of replacing skilled staff coolly poached by monetary inducement on to a rival's payroll.

The surprising thing is not that the adoption of the latest equipment caused problems, but that its implementation was sufficiently advanced for the deadline of 27 October 1986 to be met with relative ease. On that date it was not the member firms which faltered but the Stock Exchange's central SEAQ system. However, October 1986 marked not a conclusion but a mere beginning. The doubt must be whether firms will all be able to sustain the technical pressure when the FSA becomes fully operational in 1988. By then thousands of new rules will at last have been cleared by the SIB/SRO bureaucracy, and the electronic systems which have been geared to handle computer-driven stock dealings will have had to be amplified to comply with the new procedures — for many of which the rules, even if drafted, are not yet promulgated.

The essential systems today for firms engaged in brokerage and/or market-making are those that cover the four basics. These are:

(a) to deliver comprehensive information on the state of the market:
(b) to reflect all relevant deals as they occur;
(c) to provide a mass of lateral and background data to meet what might be called 'risk management'; and
(d) to cope with the administrative aftermath of accounting and settlement, the vital 'back room' operation.

Ideally these four systems are linked, but in practice it usually proves necessary to instal them separately. Actual installation can be simple; what is invariably difficult is to correlate incompatible systems and to find and retain competent operating staff.

In professions where information represents opportunity, and opportunity money, the instantaneous availability of computer-driven data does not necessarily offer accelerated profit, since others can share it, but it certainly offers enhanced risk, since deprivation of information is opportunity forfeited. A single computer breakdown could cause immediate heavy loss; successive breakdowns could destroy a firm. It has always been possible for firms to fail through inefficiency, bad management or unlucky judgment, but failure through electronic fault is a new hazard, and the ratchet is all one way: good technology will not necessarily make anyone succeed, whereas bad technology will decidedly make some go under.

The present technological adaptation in London is far more extensive, and has been far more rapid, than that experienced in New York after 1975, and the sophistication of the two leaps forward is not to be compared. That the leap undertaken in London was fully justified has been proved by what happened immediately after Big Bang: the floor of the Stock Exchange quickly and dramatically emptied and, apart from traded options dealers, has remained empty. The speed of transition to a distributed market astonished everyone.

Technological Systems: The TOPIC Base

Though the process of technical growth in 1984-86 was very rapid it was not from a zero base. There already existed, under Stock Exchange auspices, a foundation to build on. Its two main features were a database called EPIC, and an on-line information service called TOPIC which had grown out of systems of some fifteen years standing.

TOPIC was an extensive private 'viewdata' system channelling in colour a variety of information on some 20,000 'pages' to over 3000 terminals in Britain. At the source end was a dedicated connection with the Stock Exchange's central computers, including standby lines to ensure continuity. At the terminal end was an adaptability to either TV or computer, and to a printer link for copying any screen display.

TOPIC offered a variety of displays, including:

(a) the prices of some 2300 leading equities and gilts;

(b) the prices of traded options, of many stocks on the unlisted securities market, and of a widening range of international securities, especially after the inauguration of SEAQ International in 1985;

(c) company announcements as posted on the trading floor of the Stock Exchange;

(d) commentaries, analyses and forecasts both from the Exchange's own economic service and from private consultants;

(e) foreign exchange and money market rates.

Though most of this data on TOPIC could not be 'real-time information', it was frequently updated—in the case of one key indicator of leading stock prices, the 'FT-SE 100 Index', every sixty seconds. It was therefore a system that attracted subscribers from a much wider catchment area than merely Stock Exchange membership: bankers, accountants, corporate treasurers, fund managers and local authorities were among those for whom it was a worthwhile tool.

Technological Systems: The SEAQ Overlay

The inception of SEAQ International in June 1985, mentioned as tantamount to a 'second Little Bang' under 'Consequence Two' in Part Two, was indeed a significant step. It was a rational progression in four regards:

(1) In providing a London-based network for trading international equities, it recognised that whereas in the past an efficient market 'floor' was the forum for all transactions, in the future it would be the electronic coverage of a time zone that mattered most.
(2) It exploited the unrivalled advantage that the City had in its experience of international stock dealing (as compared with New York and Tokyo which have always been predominantly domestic markets).
(3) It recognised that investors with diversified portfolios in leading foreign equities, inevitably influenced by the new fluidity in currency and commodity supply, would demand access to instantly available real-time quotations.
(4) It anticipated a 'globalising' trend towards the widest possible dissemination of prices and disclosure of dealing, by networking its prices into other systems than TOPIC: e.g. Reuters, NASDAQ and several more.

The most obvious advance SEAQ International offered, over the viewdata already in TOPIC, was in displaying the simultaneously competing quotations of rival market-makers. By reference to composite 'pages' covering each stock, the investor was enabled to monitor two-way prices. All prices were already grossed to include any commission element, so the comparison was a clear one. Most prices were 'firm', i.e. they offered a basis for immediate dealing (for a given minimum number of shares, which was stated on the display). Each of the three 'regions' initially covered, namely North America, Europe and the Far East, was opened for firm-price dealing during pre-set and agreed hours, and there were likewise mutually agreed conventions governing post-transaction settlement. What began as a pattern of dealing etiquette was gradually formalised into a Rule Book as the market, initially administered ad hoc by the Stock Exchange's International Markets Committee, moved towards emergence as a full-blown Recognised Investment Exchange (RIE) under the Securities Association (see Appendix C).

The introduction on 27 October 1986 of the full SEAQ service (i.e. London-derived SEAQ Gilts and SEAQ Equities in addition to the already existing range of SEAQ International) was therefore not so much a revolution as an extension of an innovation that had already had more than a year's trial.

However, it did prove traumatic, because

(a) in heralding a shift away from traditional floor dealing, it compelled all existing and intending market-makers and all major brokers to make a heavy investment in new technology and to apply themselves painfully to learning how to use it; and

(b) it broke down spectacularly on the very first day.

However it is now clear that SEAQ works well: the emptying of the Stock Exchange floor is sufficient evidence. Even in its first month SEAQ operated at 97% efficiency, a standard regarded as normal for its American equivalent, NASDAQ. It was unfortunate that on 27 October 1986 there were twenty television crews and a hundred journalists in the Stock Exchange gallery, so the technical breakdown could not have occurred at a better-publicised moment.

Since it has sometimes been suggested that the Stock Exchange authorities are resistant to change, an instance where they were ahead of their own practitioners is to be noted. They accurately foresaw that the introduction of SEAQ portended the almost immediate end of traditional trading methods for equities and gilts. The market-makers and brokers doubted this, and it was on their initiative (and at their expense, some £3.5m) that before Big Bang the floor was specially wired for the installation of screens, as an on-the-spot adjunct to face-to-face transactions. Soon after 27 October 1986 the floor was nearly empty and the more far-sighted view of the authorities was vindicated.

SEAQ is, in effect, a series of Digital Equipment Corporation VAX 'super-mini-computers', and as such a fairly sophisticated new facility grafted onto the existing TOPIC network. The flexibility of what it is at present able to offer is well illustrated by the SEAQ Equities service. This gives prevailing prices, up to the minute, on nearly 4000 equities, which are graded as follows according to the frequency with which they are traded:

- *Alpha stocks.* These, a few score of the most actively traded equities (less than 2% of the number of stocks quoted), represent 75% of the Exchange's daily turnover. For Alpha stocks, all trades are published immediately and all prices are submitted on a two-way basis and taken as 'firm' as soon as keyed in.
- *Beta stocks.* These are over 500 less actively traded equities. With them, trades are recorded less immediately

but are likewise on a continuous two-way footing, and firm.

- *Gamma stocks.* These are over 3000 relatively inactive equities. Though continuous two-way quotes are still shown the prices are regarded as 'indicative' rather than firm.

So much for the subject coverage of the service. Its distribution to contributors is on three levels, listed in ascending order of comprehensiveness, as follows:

- *Level 1* (investor service). This service extends through Britain and Ireland to the USA, and is for the 'investment community outside the Stock Exchange', whether institutional or private, as well as for member firms. It displays, on TOPIC, a 'single best quote' for each Alpha and Beta stock, and in the case of Alpha stocks supplementary information on the day's cumulative trading position.
- *Level 2* (competing quotations service). This service, available in Britain and Ireland, shows to TOPIC subscribers, whether Stock Exchange members or not, the competing bid and offer prices on all leading equities, with supplementary information on Alpha stocks.
- *Level 3* (market-maker input service.) This is a service confined to market-makers, who are enabled by it to input their two-way prices for the stocks in which they are registered traders, and to report their trades. They do this in special input terminals designed by the Stock Exchange. From that input is compiled the up-to-date best-price and (for Alpha stocks) last-deal information, thereafter channelled to the TOPIC network.

The SEAQ Gilts service can be more simply outlined. It is available to members and non-members alike, in Britain and Ireland, and provides on TOPIC a real-time price display for most gilt-edged stocks and bulldogs. It also provides an alphabetical gilts index, showing the names of market-makers prepared to make two-way prices.

SEAQ represents a step towards an ideal system, not yet devised, whereby all prices in all stocks will be communicated simultaneously to all market-makers, while permitting them to modify the given data instantaneously as they key in their quotes and their deals. It is difficult to doubt, in the present exponentially-advancing state of the art, that a close approximation to that objective will one day be attained. Meanwhile, though SEAQ compares creditably with any such technology elsewhere in the world, it remains subject to faults. These, though often only short interruptions, occur more frequently than is publicly acknowledged. Their causes are twofold:

(1) The potential sophistication of SEAQ is inhibited by the comparative crudeness of TOPIC. The latter will display the latest price as and when the market-maker presses the request button. However, if he needs time to reflect or consult, he can only ascertain if that price has changed again by pressing the button again. Anxiety over best execution may impel him to do so. Such repeated requests choke the system, and the Stock Exchange has been criticised for not anticipating this.

(2) Each time a market-maker reports a communication fault the Stock Exchange is apt to suspend the relevant part of the system, so as not to handicap an individual. SEAQ itself has a standby computer but the fault commonly lies within TOPIC. In time, with modifications of TOPIC, a system may emerge that is both less prone to fault and more capable of coping with the sudden sharp surges of dealing volume that the release of important news provokes, but that time is not yet.

Technological Systems: Extensions and Supplements

Though SEAQ is a major innovation which has become widely known, it is only a stage towards the comprehensive system of technology increasingly in demand to meet the four basic desiderata that have been listed on page 68. To meet the fourth of those, back-room settlement, it is at present supplemented by TALISMAN, an acronym which rather improbably stands for 'Transfer Accounting, Lodging for Investors, and Stock Management for Jobbers'. This is an electronic settlement system, operated by a Stock Exchange agency called SEPON Ltd. TALISMAN processes all purchases and sales, commonly between 10,000 and 20,000 a day when times are quiet, and records them on a central computer. This automatically transfers ownership from seller to buyer in its records, calculates tax dues and generates the necessary paperwork. In the summer of 1987 the large backlog in backroom settlement documentation received much publicity. It can be attributed partly to increases in ordinary trading since Big Bang, partly to the massive volume of transactions caused by privatisation. TALISMAN is far from a perfect system, but the Stock Exchange have been very defensive about it and laid the blame for the backlog on their members and on company Registrars.

Anyway TALISMAN is due soon to be superseded by a much more refined electronic record system called TAURUS, which is intended to replace all paper share certificates by computerised records. Similarly the present mode of execution of a deal, which is normally by telephone, is due to be replaced by SAEF (SEAQ Automated Execution Facility), which will enable many simple or routine deals to be carried through when triggered by electronically-fed data, without human involvement beyond prior programming, and with immense economy of effort. Both these systems are still experimental, and neither is yet operative. However, plenty of other supplementary systems are already in use and are regarded by their users as indispensable.

This is mainly because of a simple factor: when SEAQ transmits 'Level 2' data on to members' screens, displaying the competing quotations that prevail on given stocks (and supplemented by the new phone-in Teleshare system), that information is simultaneously available to all readers equally, and if they had nothing else they would be in a 'level pegging' position. Their next step, accordingly, if they wish to make a competitive decision, must be to analyse and develop the data most relevant to the area in which they wish to trade. This is to meet the third of the four basics mentioned above.

To this end, most major firms have acquired SEAQ-compatible computer systems, with which to interface with SEAQ, and to refine and augment its and TOPIC's broadcast data, so as to identify any competitive advantage that may exist. Their evaluation of exposure and risk, using graphics and other analytical tools supplemented by such market intelligence and statistics as are available, is done with variously acquired data — for instance obtained in-house or externally through agencies such as Reuters and Telerate. Some firms, such as Chase Manhattan and Union Bank of Switzerland/Phillips & Drew, have privately developed entire analytic systems of their own.

(Some have also placed their 'back office' and settlement procedures on to agency-operated software, from leading specialists in computerised stock-processing.) Others however, mostly smaller firms, are content at present to survive on a manual basis without electronic interfacing with SEAQ.

In the longer run, the trend is unmistakably towards self-developed computer capacity — given a continuing increase in electronic sophistication and a continuing decline in hardware price. Self-help has incomparable advantages, in precise adaptability to a firm's internal structure, flexible trading priorities and security needs, including Chinese walls. As an example of technological advance, there now exists a tested computer capability for monitoring key 'indicators' that influence 'benchmark' stocks, and for automatically adjusting price quotations to correspond. Such prices would at first probably be indicative rather than firm: still, it is a further shift towards more automated dealing, which must increasingly be the shape of things to come. The contrary supposition however remains that the human element in dealing is ultimately irreplaceable for all except relatively simple decisions; also that London's geographical advantage in worldwide trading, in happening to overlap with the far east in the early morning and the far west in the late evening, need not be seriously eroded by the growing flexibility of automation, and the dawning potential of artificial intelligence. From the national standpoint one must hope it is so.

Conclusion

Some topics lend themselves to a neat conclusion. This one does not. The Bigger Bang, a convulsion that all can see, is not yet over, has probably hardly begun, and not till late 1988 will the regulatory implications for large sectors of the insurance and investments industry begin to have an impact. The outlines of this revolution are still too fluid and indeterminate, its consequences too oblique and questionable, for tidy definition, and there is a risk of anticlimax in attempting to provide it.

The most that can helpfully be said by way of synopsis is as follows. The Stock Exchange's Big Bang of 1986 came about in a manner that was quite as much fortuitous as foreseen. However, once a certain preliminary stage had been reached, marked by the Parkinson/Goodison agreement of 1983, various consequences began to flow, and even to look obvious. Without too much warping of a highly complex pattern of causation, these can be described in linear terms, and that is how they are summarised, as the five so-called 'consequences' listed in Part Two. However, they did not occur in a vacuum, and it would be intellectually dishonest to exaggerate the simplicity of the linkage that connected them. They occurred against a background of new and potent forces, e.g.

(a) a widely-prevailing tendency to de-regulation;
(b) developments in computer science that offered a major expansion of capability;
(c) British Government policies that favoured wider share ownership and therefore better investor protection.

They also occurred at a time when certain institutions and individuals were ready to make changes of direction, e.g.

(d) the Bank of England, prompted by a number of City stresses and scandals in the preceding decade, had come

round to acceptance of a need to move away from informal self-regulation towards greater authoritarianism;
(e) the banks, chastened by past misadventures with sovereign debt and intensely worried by growing competition from various quarters and particularly Japan and the U.S.A., were disposed to be interested in entering the dealing area of the Stock Exchange;
(f) some merchant banks, after watching the post-1975 experience of New York, were willing to embark on American-style investment banking on a broader basis;
(g) the British Government was anxious to improve the City's tarnished image and to reform its institutions as radically as necessary;
(h) the Stock Exchange had a Chairman prepared to stimulate it out of a certain besetting parochialism into a more competitive international posture.

In these relatively favourable circumstances the Stock Exchange in 1983-1986 juddered steadily, if unhappily, towards the biggest transformation in its history. At every stage it became more apparent that by abolishing the barriers and reforming the system of one institution the authorities would be permanently altering many others (for instance, by allowing dual capacity and encouraging securitisation they would destroy the former division of labour). This is what is happening, and that is the unfinished revolution which this study has sought to outline.

The implications, being unprecedented, invite some anxious questions. However the process, being uncompleted, provides as yet few answers. Among the most important questions, with which to end, are the following:

(1) *The burden of rules.* Has the City revolution brought with it an intolerable burden of new regulation? May this, and the concomitant cost of compliance, discourage smaller companies, hitherto an important and often innovating element in the financial services industry, from continuing to participate? Have the watchwords of 'investor protection' and 'disclosure' provoked over-regulation which will drive markets overseas?
(2) *The inelasticity of costs.* The next question takes account of various factors: (a) space in the City being excessively expensive; (b) technological hardware being both

expensive and quickly obsolete; (c) such costs and staff salaries being unresponsive to reductions in business volume; (d) increased competition having generated excess capacity which, with lower commissions, puts under-capitalised firms at risk. The question is, when the market turns downward, will many enterprises, which have got by since October 1986 because the scale of securities dealing has increased, go to the wall?

(3) *The risk of computer failure.* Does not every firm face a real risk of heavy loss – even, for small firms, of insolvency – due entirely to chance computer collapse? Even if the problem is no more than temporary technical illiquidity such as struck a major American bank to the apparent extent of $20 bn in 1985, might not the repercussions prove widely damaging to confidence?

(4) *The maintenance of confidence.* Will securitisation (notably the increasing involvement of other financial institutions in roles previously performed by banks) erode the fiduciary element which was once a key feature of transactions with banks? Does it increase the risk, especially when the present securities boom ends, of a loss of depositor confidence, which may one day induce by contagion a 'systemic shock'?

(5) *The control of ethics.* The final question takes account of the fact that the old close-knit configuration of the City has disappeared, being replaced by a heterogeneous international patchwork of institutions with limited loyalty to traditional club values; also that globalised and computerised dealing is difficult to monitor. The question is, since there are now many more players, and since new regulations have created more criminal possibilities, what prospect is there of keeping City fraud within bounds?

These are a few of the questions which stem directly from the City's *internal* decisions and developments that constitute its current revolution. The answers lie in the future, but what may be warning signs about confidence are already visible, with even some major participants displaying nervousness about staying in gilts and equities dealings.

Other equally cogent questions stem from *external* factors, e.g. what are Japanese intentions? What implications does the American deficit have for the world's economy, and the City's buoyancy? Might the next generation of technical equipment, superseding that now in place in London, and perhaps overriding London's time-zone advantage, be installed with equal ease in another monetary centre?

From the British national standpoint the ultimate question hinges on all those adumbrated above, and no doubt on others that have yet to raise their heads. It is whether the City of London, with its unique and splendid commercial history, its unequalled record of integrity, of past expertise and of present adaptability, will have the resilience and the resources to rise to the demands of the future, and to secure for itself and for this country an abiding position as a focus of the world's finance.

Appendices

APPENDIX A

Some Examples of Stock Exchange Cross-Ownership in the City

(A) Banks and Merchant Banks — UK	Approximate Capitalisation (£m)	Affiliation or Purchase in Whole or Part
Barclays	3,600	de Zoete & Bevan (S) 1984 Wedd Durlacher Mordaunt (J) 1984. Barclays Merchant Bank (sub)
Midland	1,300	Samuel Montagu (sub) W. Greenwell (S) 1984
Nat West	3,750	Fielding, Newson-Smith (S) 1984 Bisgood Bishop (J) 1984 County Bank (sub)
Barings	N/A	Wilson & Watford (J) 1984 Henderson Crosthwaite (S) 1984
Hambros	400	Strauss Turnbull (S) 1984 Mann & Co. (E) 1986 Bairstow Eves (E) 1986
Hill Samuel	350	Wood Mackenzie (S) 1984
Kleinwort Benson	500	Grieveson Grant (S) 1984 Charlesworth & Co. (J) 1984

Mercantile House	250	Laing & Cruickshank (S) 1984 Alexanders Discount (D) 1984 Jessel Toynbee & Gillett (D) 1984
Morgan Grenfell	700	Pember & Boyle (S) 1984 Pinchin Denny (J) 1984
N.M. Rothschild	N/A	Smith New Court (J) 1983 Scott Goff Layton (S) 1984
Schroders	175	Helbert Wagg/Anderson Bryce Villiers (S) 1984
S.G. Warburg (Mercury International)	400	Akroyd & Smithers (J) 1983 Rowe & Pitman (S) 1984 Mullens (S) 1984

Key to abbreviations

D = Discount House
J = Jobber
sub = Subsidiary
E = Estate Agency
S = Stockbroker

(Source: press. Validity: Autumn 1986. E. and O.E.)

(B) Banks — Overseas	Approximate Capitalisation (£m)	Purchases in Whole or Part
Chase Manhattan	2,000	Laurie Milbank (S) 1984 Simon & Coates (S) 1984
Citicorp	5,000	Vickers da Costa (S) 1983 Scrimgeour Kemp-Gee (S) 1984 Seccombe Marshall & Campion (D) 1985
Merrill Lynch	2,310	Giles & Cresswell (J) 1985
Security Pacific	1,750	Charles Pulley (J) 1984 Hoare-Govett (S) 1982 Campbell Neill (S) 1986 Trevor Matthews & Carey (S) 1986
Shearson Lehman/ American Express	8,810	L. Messel (S) 1984
ANZ	650	Grindlays (sub) Capel-Cure Myers (S) 1985
Crédit Suisse (& CSFB)	5,130	Buckmaster & Moore (S) 1985 Harold Rattle (J)
Hongkong and Shanghai	2,150	James Capel (S) 1984 Allied Provincial Securities (S)
Paribas	N/A	Quilter Goodison (S) 1986
Union Bank of Switzerland	8,570	Phillips & Drew (S) 1984

Key to abbreviations

D = Discount House
J = Jobber
sub = Subsidiary
M = Merchant Bank
S = Stockbroker

(Source: press. Validity: Autumn 1986. E and O.E.)

APPENDIX B

The Outline Regulatory Structure

As envisaged under the Financial Services Act 1986 [FSA]

(Still provisional in its details, unlikely to be operative till 1988)

PARLIAMENT

|

SECRETARY OF STATE, DEPARTMENT OF TRADE & INDUSTRY [DTI]

|

THE SECURITIES & INVESTMENTS BOARD LTD [SIB]
[Chairman: Sir Kenneth Berrill]

(n.b. A Marketing of Investments Board Organising Committee [MIBOC] was originally envisaged, in parallel with the SIB, to oversee the RIEs, but later the MIBOC and SIB roles were merged.)

Overseeing:

(1) SELF REGULATORY ORGANISATIONS [SROs]
(The Securities Association (SA) and others — *see Appendix C.* Division of this chart into two parts obscures the necessary lateral interplay between SROs and the most relevant RIEs, e.g. SA and Stock Exchange.)

(2) RECOGNISED PROFESSIONAL BODIES [RPBs]
(e.g. Chartered Accountants. Institutions can apply for membership if they are marginally carrying on investment consultancy business.)

(3) RECOGNISED CLEARING HOUSES [RCHs]
(e.g. ICCH; London options; Euroclear; Talisman/Stock Exchange.)

(4) RECOGNISED INVESTMENT EXCHANGES [RIEs]
(e.g. International Stock Exchange [ISE] UK & Ireland; Association of International Bond Dealers [AIBD]; London International Financial Futures Exchange [LIFFE]; London Commodity Exchange [LCE]; London Metal Exchange [LME]; Grain and Food Trade Association [GAFTA].)

(5) DIRECTLY AUTHORISED BODIES [DABs]
(The SIB would prefer to delegate all relationships, but some organisations may successfully insist on a direct link.)

APPENDIX C

The Self-Regulating Organisations [SROs]

These are to be directly answerable to the SIB (see Appendix B) and in general are to formulate Rule Books on membership, business conduct and compensation.

- SECURITIES ASSOCIATION [SA]
  This is a merger of two SROs, the Stock Exchange [SE] and the International Securities Regulatory Organisation [ISRO]. It will comprise some 250 organisations, and will regulate firms dealing, broking and advising in securities, international money market instruments, forward agreements and related options. It will have close links with several RIEs, e.g. ISE, AIBD and some overseas exchanges and clearing houses.

- FINANCIAL INTERMEDIARIES, MANAGERS & BROKERS ASSOCIATION [FIMBRA]
  This SRO will comprise some ten thousand organisations and individuals which mostly (e.g. insurance and unit trust intermediaries and investment advisers) had no previous obligation to register. Its rapid expansion to operate on that scale is posing administrative difficulties. It is a merger of two embryo SROs, the National Association of Securities Dealers and Investment Managers [NASDIM] and the Life and Unit Trust Intermediaries Regulatory Organisation [LUTIRO].

- ASSOCIATION OF FUTURES BROKERS & DEALERS [AFBD]
  This will deal with members of LIFFE, commodity exchanges and some overseas exchanges and clearing houses — essentially firms broking, dealing and advising in futures and options business.

- INVESTMENT MANAGERS REGULATORY ORGANISATION [IMRO]
  Membership of this will include merchant banks, trustees of collective investment schemes, and in-house pension fund managers. IMRO is expected to merge with LAUTRO (below).

- LIFE ASSURANCE & UNIT TRUST REGULATORY ORGANISATION [LAUTRO]
  This SRO is answerable in at least two directions: to the DTI in terms of the 'prudential' aspects of its members' operations (their margins, etc.), and to the SIB in terms of their sales practice.

Note. This categorisation of SROs is still untried and probably fluid. It suffers from two obvious shortcomings: that several SROs have confusingly overlapping functions; and that organisations offering a wide range of financial services will have to join, and be answerable to, more than one SRO.

APPENDIX D

Glossary

Common initials and acronyms referred to in the text.

ADR	American depository receipt
AFBO	Association of Futures Brokers and Dealers
AIBD	Association of International Bond Dealers
CAMIFA	Campaign for Independent Financial Advice
CCC	Competition and Credit Control
DAB	Directly Authorised Body
DTI	Department of Trade and Industry
FIMBRA	Financial Intermediaries, Managers and Brokers Regulatory Association
FSA	Financial Services Act 1986
GAFTA	Grain and Food Trade Association
GEMM	Gilt-Edged Market-Maker
IMRO	Investment Management Regulatory Organisation
ISE	International Stock Exchange
ISRO	International Securities Regulatory Organisation
LAUTRO	Life Assurance and Unit Trust Regulatory Organisation
LCE	London Commodity Exchange

LIFFE	London International Financial Futures Exchange
LME	London Metal Exchange
LOAF	Large Open-Area Floor
MIB	Marketing of Investments Board
MIBOC	Marketing of Investments Board Organising Committee
NASDAQ	National Association of Securities Dealers' Automated Quotations
NYSE	New York Stock Exchange
OFT	Office of Fair Trading
PFIA	Prevention of Fraud (Investments) Acts 1939 and 1958
PINC	Property Income Certificate
PSBR	Public Sector Borrowing Requirement
RCH	Recognised Clearing House
RIE	Recognised Investment Exchange
RPB	Recognised Professional Body
SA	Securities Association
SAEF	SEAQ Automated Execution Facility
SEAQ	Stock Exchange Automated Quotations
SEC	Securities and Exchange Commission
SIB	Securities and Investments Board
SRO	Self-Regulatory Organisation

APPENDIX E

Chronology

The dates of some main events mentioned in the text

1939	Prevention of Fraud (Investments) Act passed. (Implemented 1944; consolidated in a new Act 1958.)
1956	Restrictive Practices Court established.
1969	Members of Stock Exchange permitted to sell up to 10% of their equity to any one outsider.
26 March 1970	New York Stock Exchange permits corporate membership.
1 May 1975	'Mayday' de-regulation in New York: fixed commissions abolished.
1976	Authority of Office of Fair Trading extended to service industries.
1978	Office of Fair Trading notified of complaint by institutional investors about Stock Exchange's minimum commissions.
1979	Foreign exchange controls abolished.
1981	Two crashes of investment companies, including Norton Warburg.
July 1981	Professor Gower commissioned to report on Investor Protection.

1982	Members of Stock Exchange permitted to sell up to 29.9% to an outsider.
July 1983	The Parkinson/Goodison settlement.
January 1984	The date fixed (until called off) for the case against the Stock Exchange in the Restrictive Practices Court.
1984	Professor Gower's final Report presented.
July 1984	1st 'Little Bang': members of Stock Exchange permitted to deal in foreign equities with negotiated commissions and dual capacity.
January 1985	Government's White Paper on Investor Protection, etc.
May 1985	Deadline for applications to be GEMMs in Gilt-Edged Market.
June 1985	2nd 'Little Bang': SEAQ International inaugurated.
7 June 1985	5th (as described in the text) 'Little Bang': establishment of the Securities & Investments Board Ltd.
December 1985	The Financial Services Bill before Parliament.
1 March 1986	3rd 'Little Bang': Members of Stock Exchange permitted to sell up to 100% to an outsider.
July 1986	4th 'Little Bang': market in Bulldogs opened to dual capacity dealing.
27 October 1986	Big Bang.
7 November 1986	The Financial Services Act 1986 becomes law.
1 April 1988 (?)	Full functional implementation of the SIB.

APPENDIX F

The Japanese Presence in the City

Though Japan in the past twenty years has proved to be a formidably successful trade competitor in many sectors of manufacturing, the Japanese have not shown comparable skill in the export, or deployment abroad, of their financial services, where their performance has suggested either structural weakness or lack of confidence. That this situation is now changing fast is the theme of a recent book, *The Second Wave* by Wright and Pauli (Waterlow, 1987).

Japanese intentions in London remain enigmatic, but conclusions can be drawn from certain facts illustrative of the great scale, now increasing further, of their presence in the City. For instance, by early 1987 the four leading Japanese securities houses now operating in Britain had recruited in the City or brought in from abroad staff on the following scale, representing a very great expansion in two years:

Nomura	500
Daiwa	400
Nikko	300
Yamaichi	300

In recent months the figures of employment in London by those four firms have further increased. Meanwhile the total of Japanese securities houses represented in the City, on varying scales of activity, has risen to over 70.

Their volume of commercial lending in Britain, until recently too low to provoke alarm, has now risen to about 25% in volume of all British banks' comparable lending. Their share of the UK Local Government Bond market is assessed at 40%. In the Eurobond market, where their position was inconsiderable four years ago, they are now dominant. Equities and gilts are judged to be their next selected target. Their impact on the property market is mentioned in Appendix G. In all these areas, what they bring to bear is massive capitalisation, which gives them the ability to bear losses while they shave prices: in a sense they can afford to dump capital, just as, in the view of their trade rivals, they have dumped consumer goods.

In this connection, a tabulation of comparative capital weight speaks for itself. In early October 1987 the market capitalisation of the four leaders was approximately as follows:

Nomura	£35bn
Daiwa	£17bn
Nikko	£14bn
Yamaichi	£11bn

The equivalent figures at the same time for the leading American investment bank and two leading British merchant banks were as follows:

Merrill Lynch	£2.5bn
Morgan Grenfell	£0.840bn
Kleinwort Benson	£0.558bn

This enormous capital preponderance extends of course to commercial banking (as *The Second Wave* illustrates vividly). Whereas in 1980 none of the five largest banks in the world in capital terms, and only one of the ten largest was Japanese, the first five are now all Japanese (Dai-Ichi Kangyo, Fuji, Sumitomo, Mitsubishi and Sanwa). To relate it to British terms, eleven Japanese banks are now larger than our largest, National Westminster, which ranks sixteenth worldwide.

Considering that over one third of all the world's bank assets are now in Japanese hands, and considering that the recent comparative slowing-down of Japan's internal and industrial economy has the predictable effect of diverting surplus Japanese capital all the more urgently into overseas lending, we can appreciate that the City of London's recent structural revolution, and Britain's currently buoyant economy, have provided a timely opening for the dispersal of Japanese funds in search of an outlet. What we cannot at present judge is how far the process will go, and with what consequences for our home-grown firms and institutions.

APPENDIX G

The Property Market

The market in property is a complex and fluid sector to assess, and there is no ideal moment for doing so. However, this book, describing an incomplete revolution, would itself be incomplete if it failed to provide some general overview of the highly relevant property factor: it is now becoming possible to trace certain measurable, not to say conspicuous, developments that have occurred in the twelve months since Big Bang.

There have been references in the main text to the steeply mounting cost both of office sites in the City and residential property in the London area. Neither factor is exclusively attributable to Big Bang or its aftermath. Earlier considerations, notably the boom in foreign exchange and Euro-dealing, and the inrush of foreign bankers, generated an active property market, and in the eleven years 1976-86 the capital value per square foot of commercial property in the City rose from about £200 to nearly £800, with a fairly steady annual increase of about £55. However, the indications are that by the end of 1987 the capital value will have risen dramatically to over £1200, a sudden jump of £450 in one year. Throughout Britain the commercial property market is now seen to be 'stronger' (a euphemism meaning worse, for those who buy or begin to rent) than for half a century or more. Average rentals across the country are loosely estimated to have risen by 18% in the twelve months since October 1986, but the City figure will predictably come out much higher, and will contrast strongly with the average compound growth rate of some 7% since 1970. In one well-publicised contest that ended in September 1987, when the Mountleigh Group gained control of the Pension Fund Property Unit Trust, it emerged that the valuation of the Trust's City properties had in effect gone up in the previous six months by no less than 44%.

Given this upward trend, it is no coincidence that 'unitisation', a new and experimental mode of property dealing, is now being evolved. Its purpose is to increase the liquidity and flexibility of property as an investable commodity, by fragmenting large and expensive buildings and complexes into manageable units represented by shares: these are to be offered for trading on the Stock Exchange, employing the same modalities (SEAQ, Talisman, etc) as other more normal stocks. This innovation, due for launch in April 1988 when County Bank and Richard Ellis Financial Services offer shares in a single London commercial building, will take the form of PINCs (Property Income Certificates); other deals, and possibly other forms of instrument, are expected to follow shortly. The promoters of unitisation claim, persuasively, that by capturing the attention of investors and displaying improved liquidity, the system will come to have repercussions beyond London, for instance in the renewal of decayed inner city areas.

Meanwhile excessive demand (leading to fierce competition and commonly to tendering for occupancy on a 'best offer' footing) is a principal cause of cost inflation, and in the City it is not expected to be overtaken by adequate supply before 1989 or 1990. This is partly because delays in the processes of purchase and planning consent have greatly reduced the square footage of office space coming on to the market during 1988, from the previously expected 5m to a probable 3.5m square feet. However, property surveyors' estimates suggest that 8m square feet will be developed in 1989, of which the greater part already has planning consent, and a substantial proportion has even been pre-let. The delays in 1986/87 are attributed to the developers' general under-estimate of the massive additional volume of accommodation required, including the Large Open Area Floors (LOAFs) now being sought as a direct result of Big Bang. The City Corporation is also blamed for only belatedly, in 1986, recognising the need to bow to pressure for new development within the City.

The Corporation were allegedly stimulated in the end not so much by the direct pressure of demand as by the clear evidence that it was being in fact siphoned off into more welcoming areas with lower rentals, notably the Docklands enterprise zone. Docklands had indeed moved in 1986/87 into a highly expansionist phase, with development proceeding fast, encouraged by several recent events: an overdue improvement in road links, the opening of the Light Railway, the takeover of Canary Wharf by the Olympia and York Group of Canada, and, in October 1987, the opening of the new 'Stolport', providing business executives with easier air access to Europe.

Another new factor exerting upward pressure on the market is a veritable invasion of the City by Japanese property companies, which have bid successfully for a number of well placed freeholds. A year ago this Japanese factor in City property was negligible: in 1987 the situation has markedly changed, and names like Kumagai Gumi, Tasei and Itoh have become familiar through the acquisition of excellent City

St Martin-le-Grand being rebuilt for Nomura) for Japanese tenants or owner-occupiers.

According to one British estate agency, Vigers, which has a department specialising in Japanese interests in the City, in more than one recent case of strenuous competition for a key site the leading three tenders came from Japanese firms. The Banco di Roma is said to have achieved sub-lettings to Japanese tenants at Guildhall House at a near-record rate of well over £60 per square foot, which has helped to bring rates around £60 into line as targets for other owners to aspire to. Indeed a much higher rate than that is inherent in the recent sensational purchase of the *Financial Times* premises at Bracken House by the Japanese firm of Ohbayashi for £143m, which could imply a capital valuation at the eccentric-sounding level of £3000 per square foot, and which at present is commercially inexplicable, particularly as there are conservationist restrictions on the development of this notable building.

Prompted by the initial question of when is a timely moment to stand back and take stock of this booming property market in the City, one may well wonder where it will all end. Demand must presumably be finite: supply will eventually catch up with it, whereupon prices will cease to rise so steeply, if at all. Other factors than saturation may play a part in this process. Improved technology may render the enormous LOAFs at present fashionable redundant. More firms than the two or three that have recently backed away from the equities and gilts markets may follow suit. Bear conditions may set in, with an immediate shrinking effect on most sectors of the City, and property values among the foremost. Meanwhile those values are expanding like a balloon. In the concluding chapter of this book two warning notes were struck, and both are relevant to property: the conspicuously dangerous inelasticity of costs, including site costs, in face of a falling market; and the enigma of Japanese intentions.

Index